a note from thie
Pimmell with cy
According to theit
Cockcroft, this i
spelling of her surname.

Our Old House
Connie Pummell

Copyright © Connie Pummell 2018

All rights reserved. No part of this publication may be reproduced, stored in a retrieval system, or transmitted, in any form or by any means, electronic, mechanical, photocopying, recording or otherwise, without the prior permission of both the copyright owner and the publisher. Constance Pummell, writing as Connie Pummell, has asserted her right to be identified as the author of this work in accordance with the Copyright, Designs and Patents Act 1988.

If you are a copyright holder and feel inclusion of your work has not been acknowledged, please advise the publisher and an acknowledgement will be placed in any future edition.

First published in Great Britain in 2016
by
Farthings Publishing
8 Christine House
Scarborough YO11 2QB
UK

http://www.farthings-publishing.com

E-mail: enquiries@farthings.org.uk

ISBN 978 – 0 – 244 – 07033 – 5

August 2018 (q)

CONTENTS

CHAPTER	TITLE	PAGE
1	Background	7
2	1770-1798	9
3	1798-1815	16
4	1815-1840	19
5	1846-1851	25
6	1852-1870	31
7	1871-1940	41
8	1940-1972	66
9	1972-1981	75
10	1982-2000	87
11	Anecdotes	101

DEDICATION:

Dedicated in loving memory of Don who helped make my life so much more interesting and always believed in me.

A gift for our daughters, Rachel and Sally.

ACKNOWLEDGEMENTS:

Registry of Deeds Northallerton.
Scarborough Library - Bryan Berryman
Borthwick Institute York
The Scarborough Evening News
Marie Belfitt and friends.
Peter Boyes
Peter J Adams
The Collectors Centre, St Nicholas Cliff, Scarborough
Joseph Brogden Baker - History of Scarborough
Scarborough Masonic Hall
Dorothy Hurrell – Owner of Number 15 St Nicholas Cliff in 2018

Snippets and a History of 14 – The Masonic Hall, and 15 - The Stewart Hotel, St Nicholas Cliff, Scarborough, built in 1793

Chapter 1 - Background

It has to be noted from the outset that the house numbers were 11 and 12 respectively in documentation and records up to 1855, when they changed to 14 and 15. This detail was found in the Will of Christopher Ling 1855.

My husband, Don, and I ran a small hotel on St Nicholas Cliff for a little over 28 years. Our charges for dinner, bed and breakfast in the summer of 1972, our first year, were £2.10 per day, for Front rooms with a view of the sea and the Grand Hotel; £2.00 per day, for Back rooms - with a view of the back yard and the back of Palm Court Hotel; and £1.50 per day for Rooms on the top floor, these being attic type sloping ceilings. This was the 4th floor of bedrooms, and no lift but the views were beautiful.

Don, in his wisdom, decided we would have to improve the top floor to generate more income. Consequently, and eventually in 1977, we started to rebuild this floor. It was taken right down to floorboard level. Whilst demolishing this area, Don found, hidden behind a partition wall, a folded hand-written letter dated 1750. He opened it very carefully realising it may be of significance. We knew it was an old building, but did not know an original date as the Deeds only went back to 1883, and the rumour was the buildings on the West side of the Cliff dated around the mid 1760's.

As it transpired, after involving the Museum, it was found that the letter was asking certain people to attend a court hearing at the sign of the 'Crooked Billet'. This was for selling alcoholic drinks without a license. We never did find where the Crooked Billet was situated. But the finding of the letter interested us both and inspired me to research the history of the building. The original Deeds had long since disappeared. With the aid of the County Archivist at Northallerton, M. Y. Ashcroft and my constant letters, over a two-year period, we located the original Deed dated 1791. It was discovered as a piece of land for sale with measurements; sold by Richard Courteen of Scalby, Gentleman to Architect William Chambers, followed by another Deed dated 1793. Whereby, the Architect William Chambers sold the buildings to the Gentlemen brothers of John and Robert Henderson, who had several houses on the Cliff.

Visitors originally came to Scarborough for the restorative and medicinal properties of the Spaw water and sea. They were known as "Spawers" between 1730's and 1820's and took to sea bathing as nature intended – naked!

Chapter 2 – 1770 - 1798

1770 Map

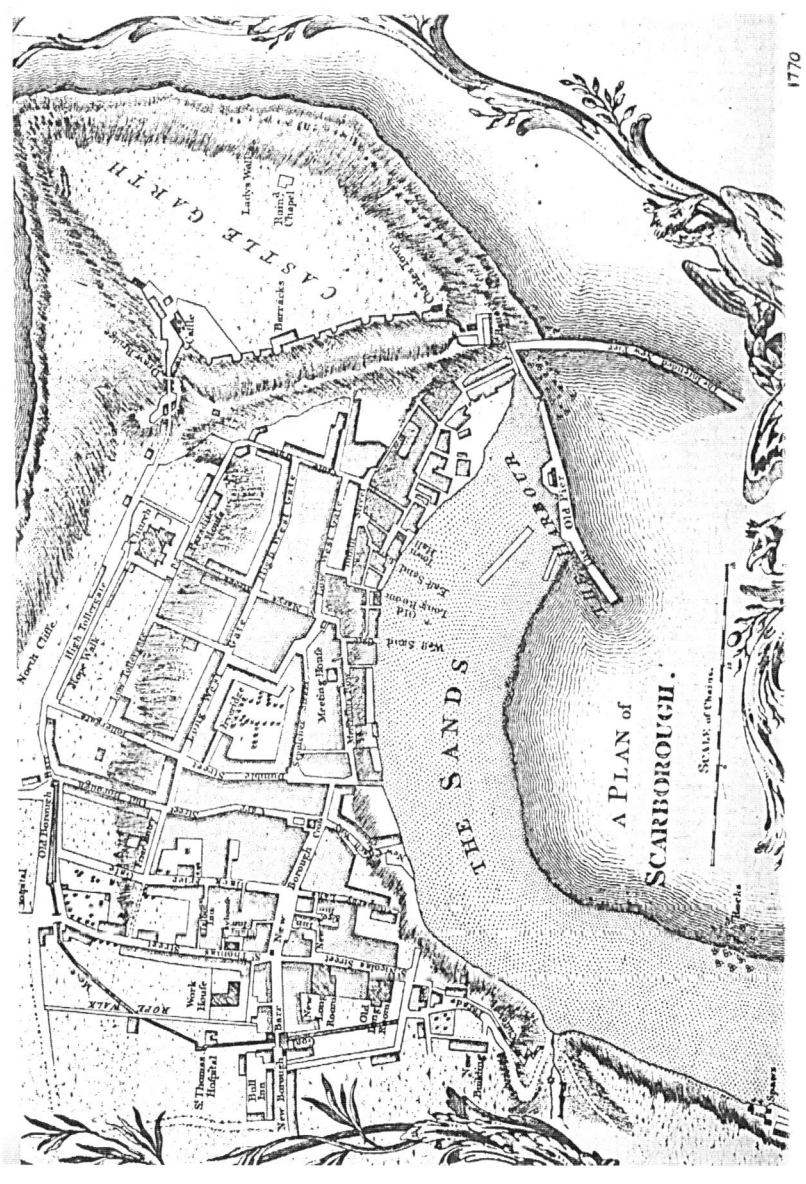

The Masonic Hall, 14 and the Stewart Hotel, 15, St Nicholas Cliff, Scarborough. A comparison of Deeds by Constance Pummell

14, St Nicholas Cliff	15, St Nicholas Cliff
1791, May, Richard Courteen of Scalby sold a piece or parcel of land, to William Chambers Architect of Scarborough.	**1791, May,** Richard Courteen of Scalby sold,a piece or parcel of land, to William Chambers Architect of Scarborough.
1793, 28th February, William Chambers sold two newly erected houses to the Gentlemen brothers of John and Robert Henderson.	**1793, 28th February**, William Chambers sold two newly erected houses to the Gentlemen brothers of John and Robert Henderson.
1815 John Henderson died and passed his properties on to his son Francis Henderson.	**1815** John Henderson died and passed his properties on to his son Francis Henderson.
1828 Robert Henderson died and passed his properties on to nephew Francis Henderson.	**1828** Robert Henderson died and passed his properties on to nephew Francis Henderson.
1839 Francis Henderson died and passed his properties on to his sister Mary Henderson.	**1839** Francis Henderson died and passed his properties on to his sister Mary Henderson.
1866, 10 August, Mary Henderson died, who had previously married a Dr. John Cockroft her name then being Mary Cockroft. She stipulated in her Will that the next person to own the properties should be called Henderson. The next owner was **Robert Henry Page Henderson**, her nephew from Beckingham, Kent.	**1866, 10 August**, Mary Henderson died, who had previously married a Dr. John Cockroft, her name then being Mary Cockroft. She stipulated in her Will that the next person to own the properties should be called Henderson. The next owner was called **Robert Henry Page Henderson,** her nephew from Beckingham, Kent.
1884 Rebecca H Henderson wife of Robert Henry Page Henderson sold to the Masonic Hall. Rebecca's address on the Deeds was Kensington London.	**1883 Rebecca H Henderson wife of Robert Henry Page Henderson** sold to Mary Hopwood of 1. Pavillion Square.
	1899 Mary Hopwood died, making a Deed of gift to her daughter Annie Hopwood.
	1920 Annie Hopwood, then 68 years old sold to Richard Kelly, a decorator. He named it Allenby.
	1927 Richard Kelly sold, Deed to Marmaduke Wesley Chapman an Accountant of Whitby.
	1931 31st December Conveyance to the Trustees of the Masonic Hall.
	1949 The Trustees of the Masonic Hall had it auctioned. Purchased by Ideal Estates of Doncaster Ltd.
	1952 Ideal Estates sold to Mr. Clifford and Mrs. Jessie Poskitt, who named it the Stewart Hotel.
	1971 Mr. Poskitt sold to Mr. Don Pummell, who then sold to Barbara Ann Keen in **July 2000.**

May 1791 - Copy of Deed

No. 692 A Memorial of Indentures of Lease and Release bearing date respectively the Thirtieth and thirty first days of May in the Year of our Lord one thousand seven Hundred and Ninety one both made Between Richard Courtson of Seaby in the County of York Gentleman of the one part and William Chambers of Scarbrough in the said County Architect of the other part and both Concerning all that Homestead or piece or parcel of Ground situate and lieing in Scarbrough aforesaid late parcel of a Close called little Saint Nicholas Close as the same is now staked or fenced and containing in front from North to South forty eight feet and Six Inches or thereabouts and from East to West ninety four feet and ____ Inches or thereabouts adjoining a private Road on the East, on another private Road on the West on Premises of the said Richard Courtson on the North and on Premises of Mr. Dobby on the South and to which said Homestead or piece or parcel of Ground was lately purchased by the said Richard Courtson along with his said Premises on the North Side thereof together with other ____ Hereditaments of Mr. Eleanor Hall of Scarbrough aforesaid and several others and also free Leave and Liberty to and for the said William Chambers his Heirs and Assigns to pass and repass to along and from the said private Road on the West side of the said Homestead or piece or parcel of Ground on foot only but to be entirely and absolutely excluded and debarred from using the same private ____ with Horses Cattle Carts and Carriages and also free Leave and Liberty for the said William Chambers his Heirs or Assigns of making a Covered Drain from the said Homestead or piece or parcel of Ground Westward to and along another piece or parcel of Ground on the West side of the said last mentioned private Road belonging the said Richard Courtson down to the Valley at the Bottom or West End thereof and so as such Drain when made be not carried further into the said piece or parcel of Ground of the said Richard Courtson than the space of three feet from the Fence of the said Mr. Dobby on the South side thereof all the Way to the said Valley doing as little damage as possible to the property of the said Richard Courtson his Heirs or Assigns either by Negligence delay or otherwise and so as the said Richard Courtson his Heirs or Assigns when such Drain shall be made by the said William Chambers his Heirs or Assigns have the like Leave and absolute right of ____ in ____ ____ ____ Drain that they shall at anytime ____ ____ ____ proper to make on to such Drain of the said William Chambers his Heirs or Assigns as shall at any time hereafter be made by him or them in manner aforesaid together with all and singular the Appurtenances thereto belonging which said Indentures are witnessed by Richard Hampton ____ ____ ____ ____ aforesaid Gentleman and William Herbert ____ Signed and Sealed ____ ____ ____ ____ Sworn

In the presence of W. Herbert

Rich Courtson

May 1791 - Transcript of Deed

Registered on the 26th March 1792 at 9 in the aforenoon

692 A **Memorial** of Indentures of Lease and Release bearing date respectively the Thirtieth and thirty first days of May in the Year of our Lord one thousand seven Hundred and ninety one both made Between Richard Courteen of Scalby in the County of York Gentleman of the one part and William Chambers of Scarborough in the said County Architect of the other part and both Concerning all that Frontstead or piece or parcel of Ground situate and being in Scarborough aforesaid late parcel of a Close called little St Nicholas Close the same is now staked and fenced and containing in front from North to South forty eight foot and Six Inches or thereabouts and from East to West sixty (not clear) four foot ... Inches or thereabouts adjoining a private Road on the East, on another private Road on the West on Premises of the said Richard Courteen on the North and on Premises of Mrs Dobby on the South and which said Frontstead or piece or parcel of Ground was lately purchased by the said Richard Courteen along with his said Premises on the North side thereof together with other " " Herediterments of Mrs Elianor Hall of Scarborough aforesaid and several others and also free Leave and Liberty to and for the said William Chambers his Heirs and Assigns to pass and repass to along and from the said private Road on the West Side of the said Frontstead or piece or parcel of Ground on foot only but to be entirely and absolutely excluded and debarred from using the same private Road with Horses Cattle Carts and Carriages and also free leave and Liberty for the said William Chambers his Heirs and Assigns of making a covered Drain from the said Frontstead or piece or parcel of Ground Westward to and along another piece or parcel of Ground on the Westside of the said last mentioned private Road belonging the said Richard Courteen down to the Valley at the bottom or West End thereof and so as such Drain when made be not carried further into the said piece or parcel of Ground of the said Richard Courteen than the space of three foot from the Fence of the said Mrs Dobby on the South side thereof all the way to the said Valley doing as little drainage as possible to the property of the said Richard Courteen his Heirs and Assigns either by negligence display or otherwise and so as the said Richard Courteen his Heirs or Assigns when such Drain shall be made by the said William Chambers his Heirs or Assigns have the privilege and absolute right of putting any drain or Drains that he or they shall at any time afterwards think proper to make into such Drain of the said William Chambers his Heirs or Assigns as shall at any time thereafter be made by him or them in manner aforesaid together with all and singular the Appurtenances thereto belonging which said Indentures are Witnessed by Richard Hampton ... ... of Scarborough aforesaid Gentleman and William Hebelthswait (?) Signed and Sealed in the presence of H. ... Sworn Affid W. Herbert   Richard Courteen   (some names not clear)

12

Engraving of the Old Wooden Spaw from Joseph Brogden Baker's History of Scarborough

28th February 1793 - Copy of Deed

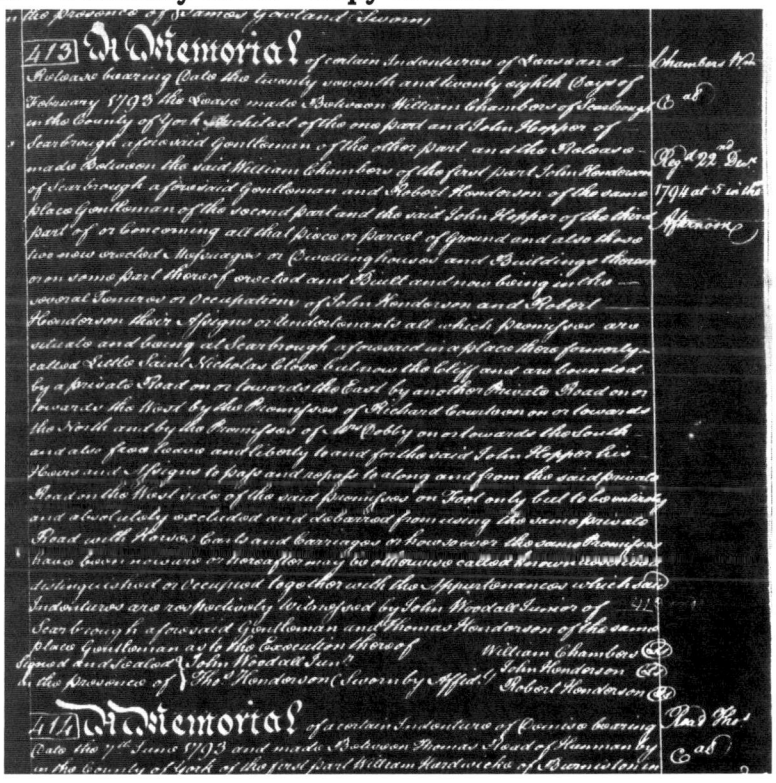

28th February 1793 - Transcript of Deed

413   Registered 22 Dec 1794 at 5 in the Afternoon

A Memorial of certain Indentures of Lease and Release bearing Date the twenty seventh and twenty eight Days of February 1793 the Lease made Between William Chambers of Scarborough in the County of York Architect of the one part and John Hopper of Scarborough aforesaid Gentleman of the other part and the Release made Between the said William Chambers of the first part John Henderson of Scarborough aforesaid Gentleman and Robert Henderson of the same place Gentleman of the second part and the said John Hopper of the third part of or Concerning all that piece or parcel of Ground and also those two new erected Messuages or Dwelling houses and Buildings thereon or on some part thereof erected and Built and now being in the several tenures or occupation of John Henderson and Robert Henderson their Assigns or undertenants all which premises are situate and being at Scarborough aforesaid in a place there formerly called Little Saint Nicholas Close but now the Cliff and are bounded by a private Road on or towards the East by another private Road on or towards the West by the premises of Richard Courteen on or towards the North and by the premises of Mrs Dobby on or towards the South – and also free leave and liberty to and for the said John Hopper his Heirs and Assigns to pass and repass to along and from the said private Road on the West side of the said premises on Foot only but to be entirely and absolutely excluded and debarred from using the same private Road with Horses Carts and Carriages or howsoever the same Premises have been now are or hereafter may be otherwise called known described distinguished or occupied together with the appertainances which said Indentures are respectively witnessed by John Woodall junior of Scarborough aforesaid Gentleman and Thomas Henderson of the same place Gentleman as to the Execution thereof Signed and sealed in the presence of }

John Woodall junior	William Chambers
Thomas Henderson (Sworn by Affid.)	John Henderson
	Robert Henderson

At the latter end of the 18th Century, Schofield's Guide of 1787 and the later edition of 1796, states, generally the price to stay at a Lodging House was ten shillings per room per week, (equivalent to 50 pence today). "Servants half price; towels and sheets included which as well as table linen, etc. are washed at the expense of those who use them – the kitchen with all utensils, both for cookery and table twenty shillings per week – servants hall ten shillings ditto – a cook expects half a guinea a week".

Chapter 3 – 1798 - 1815
1798 Map of Scarborough

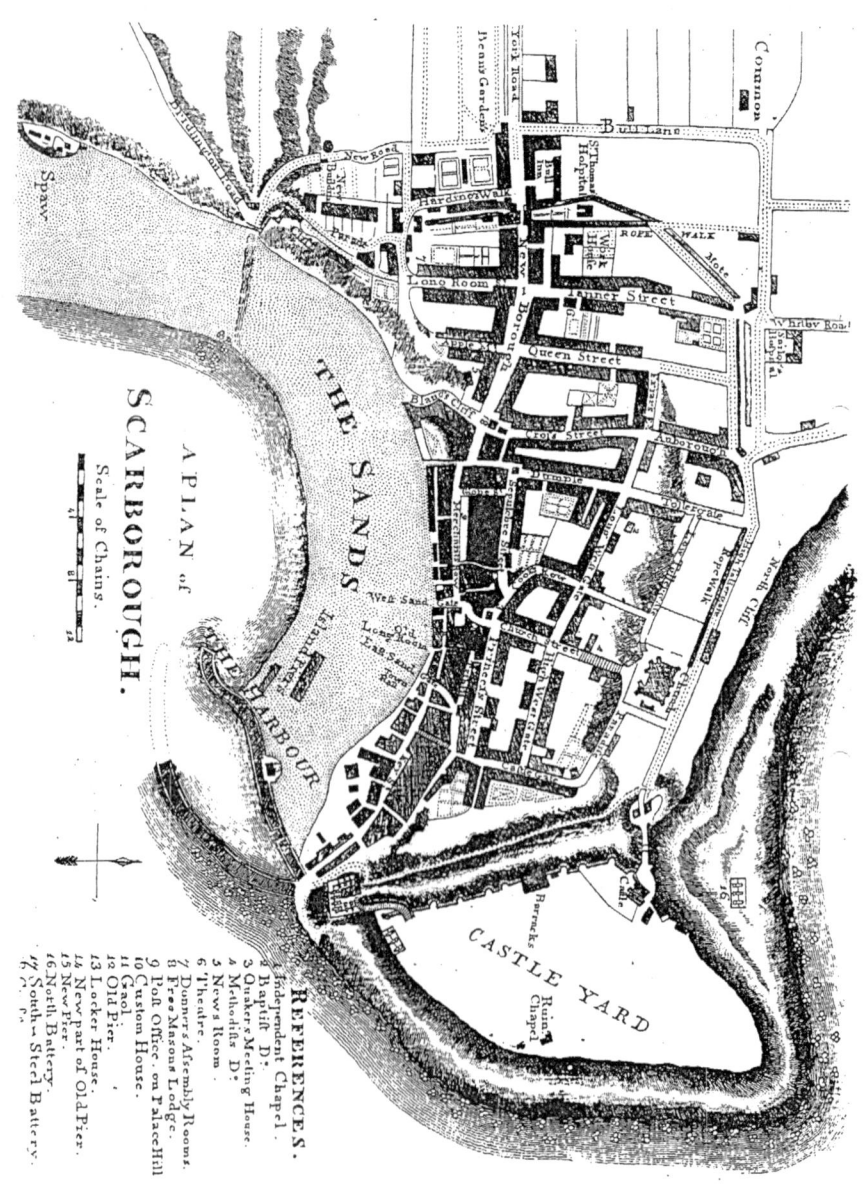

In the 1798 Hinderwell's History of Scarborough he describes: -

"The principal streets in the upper part of town are spacious with the advantage of excellent flagged footway on each side. (Made in 1775 on the Cliff). The houses have a handsome appearance particularly in Queen Street; Newborough and Long Room Street (now called St Nicholas Street), and the New Buildings on the Cliff in beauty of situation, stand unrivalled. As Lodging Houses they are commodious and elegant; and in the summer agreeably ventilated by refreshing gales from the sea. Besides the New Buildings there are many other excellent Lodging Houses in the town".

According to the Guide Book of **1806** John and Robert Henderson had "several houses on the Cliff, two of them very spacious". The early prints of the Cliff show these two houses looked very grand. At one time the Cliff was referred to as "Henderson's Cliff "because of the many properties the family owned. The Rates Books of 1837 and 1838 demonstrates this clearly.

The Poll Book of **1807**, - included on the Cliff were John and Robert Henderson, who were Gentlemen, and considered eligible to vote for a Member of Parliament.

Imagine! Take yourself back in time. Arriving by horse drawn coach, weary from the many hours of the journey, travellers having felt every bump of the rugged road. The horses were hot and steamy, ready for a rest, water and brush down in a nearby stable. There was always the threat of highwaymen on the vast open countryside between the towns.

Visitors travelled from all over the Country for this fashionable town. For visitors to stay in a Lodging House, they had to be lucrative financially, often staying for the

Season, and also bringing their servants - to look after them of course. There was none of the luxury of in house running water. En-suite facilities were chamber pots, dry toilet and commodes with the addition of ornate ceramic jug and bowl for personal ablutions. Jugs of water had to be carried up and down five flights of stairs for these ablutions. Public Baths were available throughout the town. However, probably this type of personal bathing was not carried out on a daily basis. Lashings of perfume - if you could afford them - were used to disguise fowl smelling body odours! There was no electric or gas. Coal and wood to be lugged upstairs for lighting bedroom fires and ashes carried down. Candle light or oil lamps at night – how romantic! More often, it would be early to bed and early rise, following the light of day. Feather beds and warming pans with layers of lavish warm night attire, topped off with a nightcap in winter and maybe in summer too!

1815 - John Henderson died. In his Will he named his son Francis Henderson as heir to his estate.

Chapter 4 – 1815 – 1845

Other snippets - Joseph Brogden Baker's History of Scarborough

Page 501. '1743 - Singular birthday. Mr. Henderson on the Old Cliff was born 29th February 1743, and died in 1815, aged 72, and yet was unable to celebrate more than 18 birthdays having been born in a leap year.'

Page 390. 'In 1799, the bailiffs and corporation entered into a treaty with Mr. Burg for an exchange or purchase of so much of the Long Room gardens belonging to him as might be needful of widening the road next to Mr. Henderson's house. This garden running nearly all the length of St Nicholas Street at the back of the old Town hall, had at one time the name of Bowling Green Garden.'

Page 415. 'In 1737 there were only three pleasure boats in Scarborough kept solely for the accommodation of visitors. The largest boat was 30 tons burden, called the Granby and belonged to William Henderson. It had a good cabin with bed places, so that in case of bad weather or a contrary wind springing up and detaining a party at sea all night, they could make a tolerable shift. The charge for the boat was a guinea a day.

1820s - Print of the Cliff

According to the **1821** Guide Book of Scarborough, the Lodgings on the Cliff were:

Mrs. Esther Henderson
Messrs. R. and F. Henderson, have several, two of them very spacious.
Mrs. Gowland
Mr. Sollit
Mrs. Skelton, 2 houses
Mrs. Glass
Mr. Wood
Mr. Ling
Mr. Cockerill, 2 houses
Mrs. Featherstonehaugh, 3 houses
Mrs. Peacock
Mr. Crawford, Jeweller

1827 - Guide Book. Francis Henderson had 6 houses on the Cliff.
1828 - The Will of Robert Henderson makes Francis Henderson the heir to the estate. Francis was the son of John, and was the nephew of Robert.

1828 - a part copy of the Scarborough map showing the Cliff

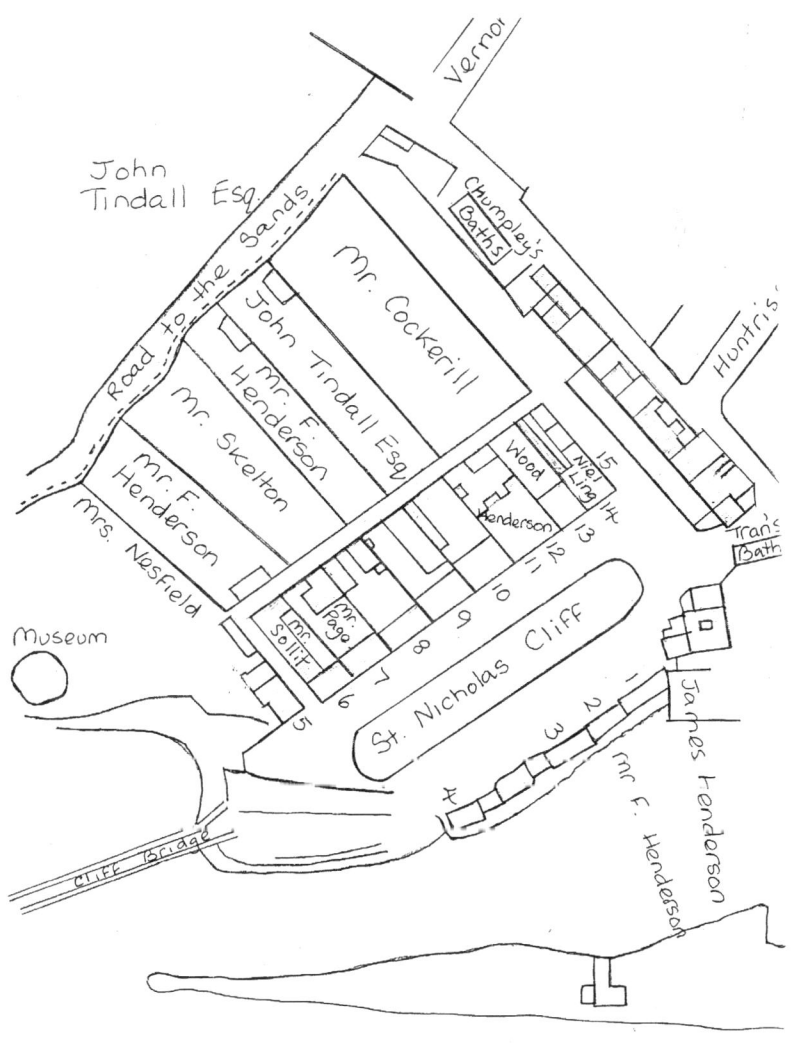

1836 Electoral List for the Cliff

Only Gentlemen were eligible to vote, Christopher Ling, John Tindall, and Francis Henderson.

House number in 1836 for these Gentlemen voters were:
16	Christopher Ling
10	John Tindall
9	Francis Henderson

1837 - Extracts from the Rates Book of 1837 demonstrates the Henderson family properties

Occupier	Owner	Property on the Cliff
F. Henderson	F. Henderson	No. 1.
"	"	No. 2.
"	"	No. 3.
"	"	No. 4
"	"	No. 9
"	"	No. 11
"	"	No. 12
"	"	No. 26
"	"	Garden, New Road
"	"	Land on Cliff
S. Prokey	"	Shop
S. Prokey	"	Shop

Extracts from the Rates Book of 1838

Occupier	Owner	Property on the Cliff
Mr. John Woodall	Mr. John Woodall	Land
Davis	F. Henderson's sister	Shop
Coldwell	"	Shop
M. Hutchinson	"	Shop
Francis Henderson	"	1.
"	"	2.
"	"	3.
"	"	4.
"	"	9.
"	"	11.
"	"	12.
"	"	26
"	"	Garden & New Road
"	"	Land
"	"	Late Raff yard
John Tindall	John Tindall (ship builder)	House (10)
"	"	Garden behind
Christopher Ling	C. Ling (in Brewing)	House (14)
"	"	House (15)
"	"	Cottage
"	"	Garden and Warehouse

1839 - Francis Henderson died on the 22 December and made his sister, Mary Henderson, heir to the family properties. Mary married Dr. John Cockroft between 1839 and 1842, but by the Census of 1851 she was a widow aged 49 years, living at 11 St Nicholas Cliff.

1840 - Print of the Cliff

Chapter 5 – 1846 - 1851

1846 - Scarborough Guide Woods Lodgings

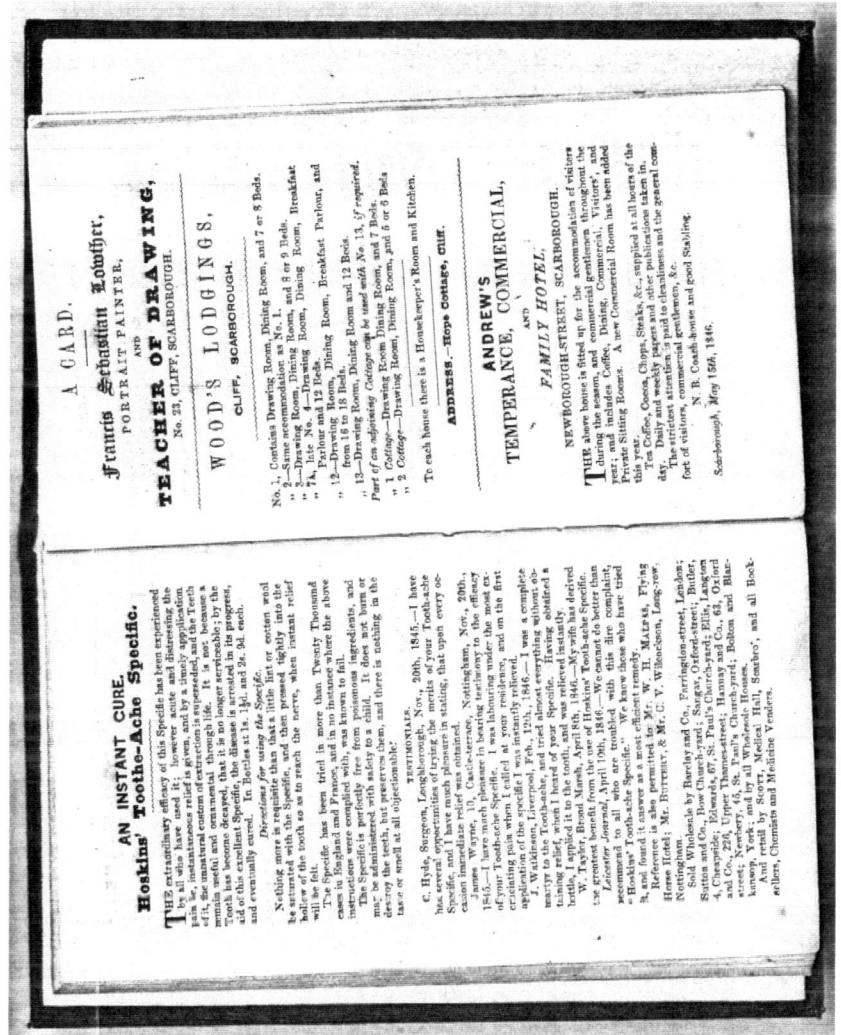

1846 - Number 12 was part of Wood's Lodgings shown in the advert in the Guide. Ann Bronte stayed at Number 2, Woods Lodgings, when she came to Scarborough, positioned where the Grand Hotel now stands. These houses were demolished from about 1862 to make way for the Grand Hotel. Ann died in 1849 and was buried at St. Mary's Church, Castle Road.

1846 - Copy of Wood's Lodgings advert in the Guide

WOOD'S LODGINGS,

CLIFF, SCARBOROUGH

No. 1. Contains Drawing Room, Dining Room, and 7 or 8 Beds.

" 2. – Same as accommodation No.1.

" 3. – Drawing Room, Dining Room, and 8 or 9 Beds.

" 7A. Late No. 4 – Drawing Room, Dining Room, Breakfast Parlour and 12 Beds.

" 12. – Drawing Room, Dining Room, Breakfast Parlour and from 16 to 18 Beds.

" 13. – Drawing Room, Dining Room, and 12 Beds.

Part of an adjoining Cottage can be used with No. 13 if required.

" 1. Cottage – Drawing Room, Dining Room, and 7 Beds.

" 2. Cottage – Drawing Room, Dining Room, and 5 or 6 Beds.

To each house there is a Housekeeper's Room and Kitchen

ADDRESS, - Hope Cottage, Cliff

1847, 1848 and 1849 - Visitor Lists for number 12. The local newspaper, The Scarborough Gazette, published Visitor Lists in the 19th Century. The following Lists are for No.12, which would be number 15 nowadays. The dates are for the week beginning and as you will see many guests stayed for quite a few weeks.

1847
Marshall, J.C. Esq., Hon. Mrs. and family, Headingly House, 19th and 26th June.
Taylor, Hy. Esq., Mrs. and family, Mote Lake 26th June.
Mildmay, Capt. G. St John R. N., Mrs. and Family, London, for 11th, 18th, and 25th September., 2nd and 9th October.
Topson, R. J. Esq. and family, Kirby Hall, near York, for 30th October.
Harcourt, Capt. O. V. and Mrs. D., Swinton Park, for 13th, 20th, and 27th November.

1848
Crompton, Sir Samuel Bart and Lady, and Misses, Woodend Thirsk, for 15th, 22nd, 29th, June, 6th, 13th, 20th, and 27th July.
Hurst, Mr. and Misses, Nottingham, for 10th 17th, and 24th August.
Mee, J. Esq., J. C. Mr., Miss and Miss M., Miss E. East Redford for 24th and 31st August, 7th and 14th September
Tetley, Mrs. and Miss, for 24th and 31st August.
Bradley, Mr. and Mrs. and family, for 31st August.
Berridge, Miss, for 31st August, 7th, and 14th September.
Gray, Wm. Esq., Mrs. and family, Gray Wm. Senior Mrs. and family for 14th September.
Hutton. Mr. and Mrs. and Mr. junior, for 14th September.

Denison, J. W. Esq., M.P. London, for 28th September and 5th October.

Heywood, J. P. Esq., and Mrs. Liverpool, for 28th September and 5th October.

Scarlett, J.W. Esq., Mrs. and family, Allerton Hill, Leeds, for 12th, 19th, and 26th October, and 2nd November.

Shiffner, t. Esq., Mrs. and family, Westergate House Sussex, for 19th, 26th October, and 2nd November.

1849

Atkinson, Mrs. Barrowby Hall, for 21st June, and 19th and 26th July.

Nainby, Mr. and Mrs. Barnoldby Le Beck, for 21st June, 19th and 26th July, 2nd, 9th, 16th, and 30th August, and 6th September.

Fraizer, Miss., for 2nd August.

Harcourt, Misses, for 2nd August.

Reed, Mrs., for 2nd August.

Babington, Mrs. and family, for 16th and 30th August and 6th September.

Elliot, Rev. C. J. and Mrs. and Family, Winkfield, for 16th, 30th August, and 6th September.

Atkinson, Mrs. for 30th August and 6th September.

Brook, Mrs. and family, Greenhead Huddersfield, for 27th September and 4th, 11th, 18th, and 25th October, and 1st November.

Howarth, Miss, for 27th September.

Riley, Mrs. and family, Huddersfield, for 27th September, 4th, 11th, 18th, and 25th October.

1850

Bowker, Mrs. Prestwick, for 8th August.

Milne, Rev. N., Mrs. and family, Radcliffe rectory, for 8th August.

Berridge, Miss, East Redford, for 12th and 26th September.
Boulton, M.P., W. Esq., and Mrs. Tew Park, for 12th and 26th September.
Mee, J. Esq.,and Misses., East Redford, for 12th and 26th September.
Postlethwaite, Mrs., Elksley Parsonage, for 12th and 26th September.
Wagstaff, MrsT., Lullington, for 12th and 26th September.
Wagstaff, T. Esq., East Redford, for 26th September.
Marshall, J. Esq., East redford, for 26th September.
Mee, J.C. Esq., for 26th September.
Maxwell, M.C. Esq., and Mrs., Dunfries, for 10th, 17th, and 31st October.
Croft, Rev. T.H. and Mrs., Hutton Bushel, for 7th November.

1851 - Census

House Number	Occupier	Position	Age
11	Mary Cockroft	Head, Widow	49 yrs
	John Hebelwhite	Footman	22 yrs
	Jane Millerton	Cook	24 yrs
	Elizabeth Christlehow	Housemaid	30 yrs
12	No one		
9	Thomas Postgate	Head, joiner	52yrs
	Jane Postgate	Wife	53yrs
	Rebecca Postgate	daughter	26yrs
	Jane Postgate	daughter	24yrs
	Henry Postgate	son	21yrs

1851 - The well-respected Surgeon, Dr. Robert Thomas Elsam Barrington Cooke lived and practiced at number 15 for more than 20 years, along with his family and many servants.

Dr. Robert Cooke studied at King's College, London where he was briefly assistant accoucheur (obstetrician). He was later House Surgeon to the Bath United Hospitals before coming to Scarborough in about 1851.

Dr. Robert Cooke was with others instrumental in the foundation of the Scarborough Dispensary in 1851, and was Honorary Surgeon to that Institution until 1878, when he was replaced. On the 1st January 1879 he was presented with a silver salver for services to the Dispensary and he was appointed Honorary Consulting Surgeon. The Scarborough Dispensary was in Vernon Place in 1853.

In 1985, his Great granddaughter Mrs. Semleyn wrote to Mrs. Connie Pummell suggesting the silver salver had been in Bright's Jewellers on St Nicholas Street, Scarborough.

Chapter 6 – 1852 -1870

1852 - Ordnance survey map of Scarborough reproduced by Peter J Adams. Section of the map including St Nicholas Cliff and a portion of the South Cliff.

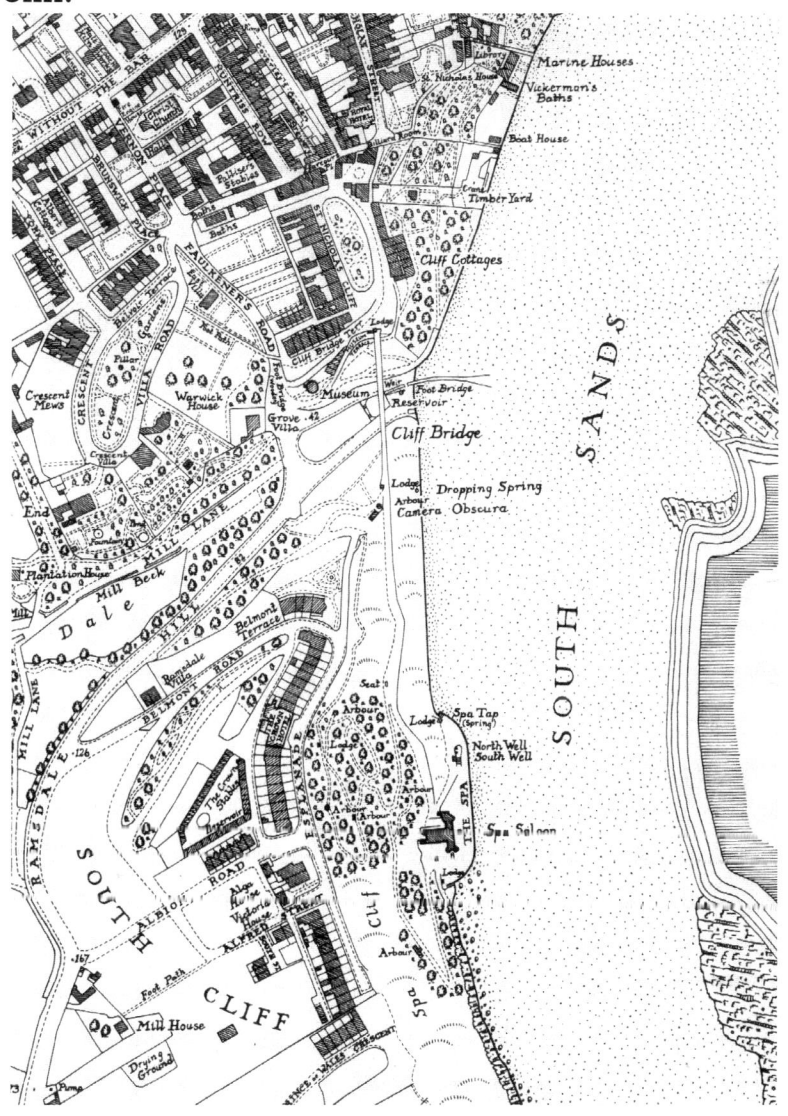

1855 - Print of St Nicholas Cliff, Scarborough

1855 - The Will of Christopher Ling
In his Will he states the house numbers had recently changed on the Cliff.

and situate upon the Cliff Scarborough aforesaid And also all that Cottage being formerly number 16 but now numbered 17 in which I now reside and situate upon the Cliff Scarborough aforesaid And also all and singular the household furniture beds bedding plate linen china books paintings pictures and portraits which may be in or about my said messuage or dwellinghouse now numbered 17 and the said Cottage in which I now dwell at the time of my decease To hold the said dwellinghouse Cottage outbuildings and premises household furniture therein unto my said dear wife Catherine During her

1859 – Extracts from the Rates Book

Occupier	Owner	Property	Gross estimated rental
Robert B. Cooke	Mary Cockroft	15. The Cliff, House	
"	"	Wash house and yard	£90.00
"	John Coates	Back of Nesfield Terrace	
"	"	Cottage, Coach house and Saddle room	
"	"	Box, Stable and yard	£17.00
William Peacock	Mary Cockroft	1. The Cliff. House and garden	£30.00
Jane Jefferson	"	2. " " "	£25.00
Jonathan Woodall	"	3. " " "	£30.00
William H Wilson	"	4. " House, cottage and garden	£95.18s
Thomas Lawson	"	5. " " "	£104.1s
Cornelius Graves	"	6. " " "	£104.1s
Shepherd D. Hudson	"	7. House and garden	£95.18s
"	"	2 Cottages 1. And 2. The Cliff	£80.00
Thomas Postgate	"	12. The Cliff, House, Cottage, Garden	
Mary Cockroft	"	14. " House, Garden,	
"	"	" Greenhouse, Coach house	
"	"	" Stables	£100.00
"	"	Land late Raff yard Sandside.	

1860 – Extracts from the Rates Book

Occupier	Owner	Description	Situation
William Peacock	Mary Cockroft	House & Garden	1 St Nicholas Cliff
Jane Jefferson	"	"	2 "
Jonathan Woodall	"	"	3 "
William H S Wilson	"	House Cottage & Garden	4 "
Thomas Lawson	"	"	5 "
"	Hannah Holmes	House & Garden	Cross Street
Cornelius Graves	Mary Cockroft	House Cottage & Garden	6 St Nicholas Cliff
Abraham Appleyard	"	House & Garden	7 "
"	"	2 Cottages	1 & 2 "
William Foy	William I Page Eps.	House Garden Yard	10 "
Henry E Hetherington.	Henry E Hetherington	House Cottage Garden } Yard & Wash house }	11 "
"	"		
Thomas Postgate	Mary Cockroft	House Cottage Garden	12 "
"	Thomas Postgate	House 2 Cottages garden	9 "
John Lilley	John Tindall's Trst.	House Garden Yard	13 "
Mary Cockroft	Mary Cockroft	House Garden } Green House Yard } Coach House & Stable} Land late Raff Yard	14 "
Robert B Cooke	"	House Wash House & Yard	15 "
"	John Coates	Cottage Coach House Saddle Room 1. Box Stable & Yard	Back Nesfield Terrace
William Dodds	William Dodds	House Cottage Yard	16 St Nicholas Cliff
Catherine Ling	Christopher Ling Exec	"	17 "
"	"	House & Yard	18 "
Matthew Tranmar	John Champley	House Cottage Yard	20 "

1861 – Extracts from the Rates Book

According to the Rates Book, although Mary Cockroft owned both 14 and 15 the Cliff, Dr. R. B. Cooke was the occupier of 15.

Occupier	Owner	Description	Situation
William Peacock	Mary Cockroft	House + Garden	1 St Nicholas Cliff
Jane Jefferson	"	"	2 "
Jonathan Woodall	"	"	3 "
William H.S. Wilson	"	House, Cottage + Garden	4 "
Thomas Lawson	"	"	5 "
"	Hannah Holmes	House + Garden	Cross Street
Cornelius Glaves	Mary Cockroft	House, Cottage + Garden	6 St Nicholas Cliff
Abraham Appleyard	"	House + Garden	7 "
"	"	2 Cottages	1 + 2 "
Mary Cockroft	Mary Cockroft	House Garden]	14 "
"	"	Green House, Yard]	"
"	"	Coach House, Stable]	"
"	"	land late Raff yard	
Robert B Cooke	"	House wash house & yard	15 "
"	John Coates	Cottage & Coach house	
"	"	Stable & Saddleroom	Back of Nesfield Terrace
"	"	Box & Yard	
William Dodds	William Dodds	House Cottage Yard	16 St Nicholas Cliff
Bejamin Green	Christopher Ling's Exec.	House & Yard	17 "
Mary Ward	"	"	18 "
Richard Sanderson	"	Cottage & Yard	19 "
John Tranmar	John Champley	House Cottage Yard	20 "

1861

Immediately after the Amelia Lifeboat disaster of the 2nd November 1861, Mary Cockroft bought the next Lifeboat for the Town called the Mary. This Lifeboat operated from 1861 to 1872, being launched 25 times and saving 32 lives.

1861 - Census

In the 1861 Rates Book Mary Cockroft owned both houses.

Number 15   **Born**

Robert B Cooke	Head	33 yrs	Apothecary	Fulford York
Emily Cooke	Wife	32 yrs		Barton Lincs.
Mary Cooke	daughter	6 yrs		Scarborough
Lucy Cooke	"	2 yrs		"
Amy Cooke	"	3 months		"
John Burg	visitor	15 yrs	nephew	
Susannah Carling	servant	18 yrs	Housemaid	Stokely
Ann Carling	servant	15 yrs	Housemaid	"
Mary A Lewis	servant	30 yrs	Cook servant	
Catherine Bulmer	servant	25 yrs	Housemaid	
Sarah Storey	servant	21 yrs	Waiting Maid	
Catherine Green	servant	17 yrs	Kitchen Maid	

Number 14

John Wright	servant	19 yrs	Footman
Hannah Banntom	servant	29 yrs	Cook/ Housekeeper

LITTLE GEMS RELATING TO THE GRAND HOTEL – FROM THE LATE MARIE BELFITT

1862 - A newly formed company – The Scarborough Cliff Hotel Company Limited – bought the Land known as Henderson's Cliff from Mrs. Mary Cockroft (nee Henderson) for £30,000. (These properties are shown in the Rates Book of 1859)

1862 (June) - The Company announced its intention to raise £120,000, in shares to "erect a large hotel, designed by Leeds architect Cuthbert Broderick".

1863 (October) - Contract to build the Scarborough Cliff Hotel, at a cost of £66,000 was let to David Climie, building contractor of Shrewsbury.

1863 (October) - Work began on construction of the Hotel.

1865 (February) - The Hotel reached 5 storeys on the low (sea) side and 2 storeys on the high (town) side.

1865 (22 August) - Dissolution of the Scarborough Cliff Hotel Co. Limited, because the company was short of capital and the contractor was bankrupt.

1865 (26 September) - The half-completed hotel and site (which had, up to then cost £90,000), was sold for £43,000 to the Grand Hotel Company Limited (a newly formed company).

1866 (January) - Work recommenced on the hotel, which was renamed the Grand Hotel.

1867 (January) - Roofing of the Grand.

In January 1867 the Grand Hotel was finally "covered in". The event was celebrated with a Roofing Dinner, in the Mechanics Institute, Vernon Place (now part of the Public Library).

A "men only" event, the dinner was financed jointly by the Grand Hotel's manager (Augustus Fricour), its architect (Cuthbert Broderick), its contractor (Archibald Neill) and its three sub-contractors, Messrs Briggs, Nelson and Walsh.

A total of 261 workmen were employed on the construction of the hotel namely:
- 31 masons and 19 masons' labourers
- 56 plasters and 14 labourers
- 78 joiners and 4 labourers.
- 8 stone carvers, 8 brick layers and 14 labourers
- 9 plumbers, glaziers and gas-fitters
- Five painters, four smiths and eight general labourers.

Two thirds of the workmen came from areas outside Scarborough, such as West Riding of Yorkshire, Lancashire, north of the river Tweed and Ireland.

Allegedly, The Grand Hotel and site cost "over £100,000". It was completed in 6 months after the Roofing Dinner and opened with a grand banquet on 25th July 1867.

1866. Grand Hotel, part built

The Spa

1866 - Mary Cockroft died on the 10th August.

In her extensive Will she stipulated that the next owner must be called Henderson, and even though she left her estate to her nephew, Robert Henry Page, he still had to change his name by Royal License within a year. Robert's address in the Deeds of 1867 was Beckinham Place, Beckinham in the County of Kent.

1867 - 14 and 15 & Grand Hotel 1867-1872

THE GRAND HOTEL, ST NICHOLAS CLIFF, SCARBOROUGH.

This print shows the Georgian frontage of 14 and 15 on the right.

Number 15 was granted plans to change the frontage to Victorian Bay windows in **1872**.

The Masonic Hall changed their frontage in **1884**.

Chapter 7 1871 - 1940

1871 - Census

Number 15

Name	condition	age	occupation	place of birth
Emily Cooke	Head	41 yrs	Wife of B. Cooke, Surgeon	Barton L.
Mary Cooke	daughter	16 yrs	Scholar	Scarborough
Lucy Cooke	"	12 yrs	"	"
Amy Cooke	"	10 yrs	"	"
Arthur Cooke	son	7 yrs	"	
Ethel Cooke	daughter	6 yrs	"	
Agnes Cooke	"	5 yrs	"	
Alfred Cooke	son	2 yrs		
Robert B Cooke	"	4 months		
Susannah Carling	servant	27 yrs	un M. Domestic servant, Nurse	
Anne Carling	"	25 yrs	" "	
Anne Bell	"	16 yrs	" Nurse	
Hannah Dent	"	23 yrs	" Domestic servant, Housemaid	
Mary Heamis	"	22 yrs	" Domestic servant, Kitchen	
Ann Warysik	"	19 yrs	" Domestic servant, Nurse	
Anne Hawkins	"	21 yrs	" Domestic servant	

Number 14

Anne Roberts	Head wid	38 yrs	Lodging House Keeper	Lincoln
Ann Roberts	daug. un M.	15 yrs	Dressmakers apprentice	Nottingham
Alice M Roberts	"	13 yrs	scholar	Nottingham
Edith B Roberts	"	5 yrs		Towse? Hull
Elizabeth Atkinson	serv. un M.	26 yrs	Domestic serv. Cook	Kirkbymoorside
Jane Pinkney	serv. un M.	21 yrs	Domestic serv. Housemaid	Brompton

41

1872 - Plans in Town Hall to change frontage of 15 to Victorian Bays

1875 - Newspaper cutting about Dr. Robert Barrington Cooke

The Scarborough Mercury- Saturday 19 June 1875
ATTEMPTED SUICIDE OF A MEDICAL MAN IN SCARBOROUGH

On Monday afternoon last a very painful incident occurred in Scarborough.

Dr. Cook , a medical practitioner , well-known and much respected in the town , while in a state of temporary insanity , attempted to destroy himself by jumping out of a third storey window of his house on St. Nicholas Cliff.

Happily , this occurred at a time of the day when many persons were about , and the unfortunate gentleman , having been temporarily restrained by some of the members of his own family , the latter were speedily assisted by several workman , who succeeded in forcing the doctor back into his own house.

This was not accomplished without some difficulty , as much determination was displayed by him to perpetuate the rash act , and it was not until the lead covering the top of the bay window had been pulled up by him that he was finally secured.

We understand that for some time past Dr. Cook has manifested symptoms of aberration of mind. Recently he lost a favourite child , and this seems to have preyed very much on his mind.

He attributed the child's death to the defective sanitary arrangements of the locality in which he resides. This impression got so strong a hold upon him that he wrote extraordinary letters to different parties , including both the Local Government Board and the Corporation of Scarborough , making the most reckless charges against the sanitary conditions of the town.

This has recently brought him into controversy with the Local Authorities , the latter of whom, it may be said , have in consequence of his accusations been induced to incur considerable expense in examining the drainage in the vicinity of the doctor's residence , only to find the drains perfect and his suspicions unfounded.

During his intercourse with Local Authorities , it is said , the doctor has conducted himself in an incoherent and contradictory manner , and this has culminated in the sad affair referred to.

We are glad to say , however , that the sufferer is progressing favourably , and hopes are entertained for his recovery.

Exact Copy From : The Scarborough Mercury - Saturday 19 June 1875 (Page 3).

1881 - Census. No-one occupied 14 and 15

Doctor Barrington Cooke, Wife and family had moved to
"The Haven", Prince of Wales Road.

Robert B. Cooke	Head	53 yrs	Surgeon
Emily Cooke	Wife	51 yrs	
Lucy Cooke	daughter	22 yrs	
Amy Cooke	"	20 yrs	
Ethel Cooke	"	16 yrs	
Agnes Cooke	"	15 yrs	
Alfred Cooke	son	12 yrs	
Robert B Cooke	son	10 yrs	
Mary Hurst	servant	25 yrs	Cooke, Domestic servant
Martha Kirk	"	22 yrs	Housemaid
Lidia Riches	"	16 yrs	Housemaid
Louise Dillibank	visitor	72 yrs	Annuant

1. Pavilion Square

Name	age	occupation	Born
Mary Hopwood Head widow	55 yrs	Lodging House Keeper,	Hunslet Leeds
Annie Hopwood daughter	29 yrs	"	Scarborough
Thomas Cuttly Lodger unmar.	47 yrs	Retail Merchant	York

1883- Rebecca H Henderson, wife of Robert Henry Page Henderson sold 15 to Mary Hopwood of 1, Pavilion Square, for the sum of £2,150.

Before moving to Pavilion Square, Mary Hopwood was listed in White's Directory as having Lodgings at 57 North Marine Road.

43

1884 - Rebecca sold 14 to the Freemasons, who altered the frontage and certain internal renovations at a cost of £1,079. Mr David Petch was the architect and the work was completed by William Peacock. These details were found in the "Flash Back" in the Scarborough Mercury.

FLASHBACK

22 February 1884

The question of opening out the communication from Huntriss Row to St Nicholas Cliff is once more prominently before the town, and it seems as though, if the present opportunity is not taken advantage of a much needed improvement will be almost indefinitely deferred. What is required is that Huntriss Row should be carried straight through to St Nicholas Cliff and that the garden in the centre of the cliff be cleared away. . .

[At that time there were houses on what is now the car-park in Falconer's Road and the north side of St Nicholas Cliff. The only entrance to St Nicholas Cliff was a narrow road opposite Bar Street. The buildings on the north side of St Nicholas Cliff remained for another ten years. The buildings on the car-park remained until the 1950s.]

FLASHBACK

The Scarborough Mercury,
AND NORTH AND EAST RIDINGS ADVERTISER
4 April 1884

NEW MASONIC HALL AT SCARBOROUGH

The Freemasons of Scarborough recently purchased the premises on St Nicholas Cliff formerly occupied by Mr Numa Blanc with the object of converting them into a Masonic Hall etc. Mr David Petch, architect, has prepared the plans, which have been adopted. At a meeting of the Building Committee on Tuesday evening tenders for the work required were considered, and that of Mr William Peacock, for the entire work, was accepted, the amount being £1,079. The work will be commenced at once, so as to be completed by August next.

1884 - Visitors Lists for 15 St Nicholas Cliff as published in the Scarborough Gazette. The dates are for the week beginning.

Aspden, Miss, Wakefield, for 26th June, 3rd and 10th July.
Brown, Miss, Wakefield, Ilkley, for 26th June, and 3rd, 10th, and 17th July.
Swindles, Miss, Ilkley,   "
Sandbach, Mrs, and family, Bradford, "
Sandbach, Rev., Bradford, for 10th, and 17th July.
Abronisberg, Misses, Birmingham, for 24th and 31st July, 7th, 14th, and 21st August.
Lyon, S. Esq., Mrs. Maid and family, Beaconsfield House Edgebaston, for 24th and 31st July, 7th, 14th, and 21st August.
Clapham, Miss., for 31st July, 7th, and 14th August.
Clapham, Mrs., Manchester, for 31st July, 7th, 14th and 21st August.
Richards, Miss., Manchester, for 31st July, and 7th, 14th and 21st August.
Whitegrove, Mr. and Mrs and family, for 14th and 21st August.
Brown, W. L. Esq., Mrs and family, Keighley, for 21st and 28th August.
Fritchie, W. Esq., and Mrs., Ashby del A Zouch, for 28th August.
Fritchie, T. Esq., for 28th August, 4th and 11th September
Fritchie, Rev. G.C. and Mrs. The Rectory, Newton Regis, for 28th August, 4th and 11th September.
Leitner, S.L. Esq., Miss and Mr. Birminham, for 28th August, and 4th September.
Taylor, S. Esq., Mrs., Southport, for 4th September.
Thatcher, J. H. Esq., and Mrs., Oldham, for 4th and 11th September

Thatcher, Miss J., for "
Thatcher, Miss L., for "
Thatcher, Miss T., for "
Thatcher, Master Robert, for "
Thatcher, Miss, Southport, for "
Waulfrum, Fraulin, for 4th and 11th September. Bladworth, Mr. and Mrs. Thos., Whitgift Hall, Yorks., for 11th and 18th September.
Darley, Mrs. Charles, Thorn Doncaster, for 11th and 18th September.
Darley, Master Francis for "
Denby, W. C. Esq., and Mrs. , for 18th September.
Catley, T. Esq., for 25th September and 2nd October.
Corker, Mr. and Mrs. for "
Cheetham, Wm. Esq., Horsforth for 2nd and 9th October.
Cheetham, Miss., for "
Cheetham, Miss E., for "
Cheetham, W. H. Esq., Guisley, for "
Lawson, A. S. Esq., London, for 2nd, 9th, and 16th October.
Lawson, Master, London, for "
Vevers, Mrs. and Mrs. C. C., Horsforth, 2nd, 9th, and 16th October.
Crowther, Mrs. and family, Huddersfield, for 9th October.
Harris, Mrs., London, for 16th and 23rd October.
Harris, Misses (2), for " Mills, Mr. and Mrs. and family, Eastfield, York, for 23rd and 30th October, 6th, 13th, 20th, and 27th November, 4th, 11th, and 18th December.
Mosely, Mr. and Mrs., Cheadle Cheshire, for 6th, 13th, and 20th November.
Mosely, Miss, for "
Mosely, Mr. W., for 13th and 20th November.

Robinson, Rev. W., for 27th November, 4th and 11th December.
Nicholson, Mr. and Mrs., Sheffield, for 4th and 11th December.
Andrew, Mrs., Sheffield, for 11th December.

1887 - Jottings Minutes from Scarborough Town Council 18th February

'At the quarterly meeting on Monday, Alderman Fowler suggested the Old Cliff, which was a disgrace to the town, should receive some attention from the Council.

The Corporation would like to buy or rent the land. Councillor W. Peacock thought the best plan was to widen the road all around by 4 or 6 feet. He thought the owners would not sell the land.

Councillor Joshua Rowntree M.P. was glad Alderman Fowler had mentioned the matter. Several years ago the Council had tried to buy the land, but the matter fell through.

The Mayor (Alderman J. W. Woodall) said he would do all in his power to assist in making improvements to the Old Cliff.

Alderman Fowler gladly concurred with these remarks made regarding the Old Cliff. There had been great improvements in that neighbourhood, particularly on the piece of land obtained from the Grand Hotel. Everyone seemed pleased with it. He suggested they sweep away the Gardens altogether and leave a space for the erection of a statue of her Majesty the Queen, which would be an additional adornment to the Town.

Councillor Petch thought it a great shame that Scarborough did not have a statue of Her Majesty.

A sub-Committee was formed to deal with improvements to the Old Cliff.'

1887 - Marriage of Claude George Henry Sitwell to Amy Elizabeth Barrington Cooke

[Certified Copy of an Entry of Marriage Pursuant to the Marriage Act 1949, recording the February 22nd 1887 marriage at the Parish Church, Harringworth, in the County of Northamptonshire, between Claude George Henry Sitwell, aged 28, Bachelor, Lieut. 85th Light Infantry, of Harringworth, father George Frederick Sitwell; and Amy Elizabeth Barrington Cooke, aged 26, Spinster, of Harringworth, father Robert Thos. Elsom Barrington Cooke.]

1887 – Minutes of Scarborough Town Council, Friday 4th March

An effort is being made to reduce the size and re-model the Gardens in St Nicholas Cliff. There is a reasonable prospect of the work being carried out in the spring.

Last November, commenting on the approaching Jubilee of the Queen, Jottings said bunting and fireworks were a waste of money. They were soon over with nothing to show for the expense. A much better use of the money would be to do up the St Nicholas Gardens as a permanent improvement, which would benefit the residents and visitors alike.

1899

Mary Hopwood died leaving number 15 to her daughter Annie Hopwood, who lived and worked with her there. Annie Hopwood would have been 47 years old.

1899 – Cutting of 'Flash Back' from Scarborough Evening News. Granby House demolished to widen the road near the Royal Hotel.

The text between the two photographs read:
'Looking along Harcourt place, Scarborough, from Kings Cliff. In the old photograph which belongs to Gibson's hotel, Queen's Parade, the Royal Hotel is on the extreme

right, and the building on the left was Granby House, demolished in 1899.' The site of Granby House is now the sunken area where Scarborough Art Society holds its outdoor painting exhibitions.

1905 - photograph of 14 and 15

1908 - Post Card, Spa Bridge

1909 - Scarborough Directory. Number 15 was classed as Apartments.

This style of accommodation was very hard work for the Landlady. Each customer brought their own food, which was stored in a locker, from which the Landlady cooked and produced meals which were then served in the dining room. Can you imagine? The Landlady must have been dizzy at the height of the season with a different meal to cook from every locker, maybe three times a day!

1914 - Bombardment

Photograph of how the bombardment affected the back of the buildings of 15, 16, and 17 St Nicholas Cliff.

The First World War "Bombardment of Scarborough" on 16th December 1914, damaged buildings on St Nicholas Cliff. The Grand Hotel took a direct hit on the East side, as did the West side of the Cliff at the back of the buildings.

1920 -

After 37 years of toiling at number 15, this unmarried lady Annie Hopwood, by then 68 years old, sold 15 to Richard Kelly, known as "Spider Kelly", a painter and decorator. It sold in 1920 for the sum of £1,450. Richard gave 15 a name, The Allenby. In the Scarborough Guide of **1923** it was described as an "Up-to-Date Boarding House". The telephone had been installed by 1924 - telephone number 265.

The Terms in the 1926 Guide were from 9/- to 15/- per day according to season. (15/- is equivalent to 75 pence in decimal coinage)

The Boarding House style of accommodation must have made the cooking a degree easier to execute compared with Apartments. But even then with a basic table d' hote menu to cook for each meal, the hours were long and the meals many!

The day began with early Morning Tea, delivered to the visitors' bedrooms: usually, by the youngest and most inexperienced of the team. Most often, the visitors were still in bed! (This practice of service of delivering early morning tea continued until the onset of the Bedroom Electric Kettle in the 1970's)

The remainder of the days nourishment and refreshments followed at a speedy pace, with the cleaning routine sandwiched neatly and methodically in between – Breakfast, Morning Coffee, Afternoon Tea, High Tea, Dinner and finally Supper. Some establishments tackled all of the Fayre, but sensibly, others axed some of the meals. It is said that Scarborough Cemetery is full of over worked Landladies.

1923 - Advert for Allenby

> ### SCARBOROUGH.
>
> **AN UP-TO-DATE BOARDING HOUSE.**
> Electric Light and Bells in all rooms.
>
> # THE ALLENBY,
> ## ST. NICHOLAS CLIFF.
> Opposite Grand Hotel and Sea.
>
> Scarborough's Premier Position for Spa, Bathing, Boating, Fishing, etc., and all Places of Amusement.
>
> Adjoining Masonic Club.
>
> Excellent Cuisine. Everything of the Choicest in season. Comfort assured. Moderate charges.
>
> Write for Inclusive Tariff,
> Mr. and Mrs. RICHARD KELLY,
> Proprietors.

Note: The Bell Board was still in the entrance in number 15 in **2000**.

Richard Kelly highlights the 'Bells in all rooms' as an asset in the **1923** advert. The Bells pushes were in the bathrooms too!

1924 – Scarborough Guide

WESTON
PRIVATE HOTEL
SOUTH CLIFF, SCARBOROUGH

FINEST POSITION ON ESPLANADE.

COMFORT ASSURED.   RENOWNED CUISINE.

PERSONAL SUPERVISION.
Mrs. WILKINSON.

Telephone 521.

"WAVE CREST"
38, ESPLANADE,
SOUTH CLIFF,
SCARBOROUGH

Private Residential Hotel and Boarding Establishment

Premier position on the Sea Front. Thoroughly Comfortable and Up-to-date.

EXCELLENT CUISINE.
TERMS MODERATE.

Telephone: Scarborough 695.

TARIFF ON APPLICATION.

Proprietress: Miss KING.

THE ALLENBY
ST. NICHOLAS CLIFF

Facing Grand Hotel, South Bay. Main entrance to Spa and adjoining Masonic Hall. Noted for homeliness, excellent catering, etc.

Everything British in season.

Country produce from neighbouring farms

Telephone No. 265.

CENTRAL FOR EVERYWHERE.

Send for Prospectus to
Proprietress:
Mrs. RICHARD KELLY.

1927 - Richard Kelly sold the Allenby for £3,900. In the Deeds this was to Marmaduke Wesley Chapman, an Accountant from Whitby.

1931 - Deed of Conveyance to the Trustees of the Masonic Hall.

However, a Mrs. F. Jones ran it as a Boarding House for a number of years, as shown in the advert for the Allenby in **1933** in the Scarborough Guide. Mrs Jones occupied the Allenby until **1937**, and then when she left she took the name Allenby with her to 23 Valley Road for the **1938** season.

1930's - Photograph of 15

This photo shows how the hotel at No. 15 would look when Mrs F Jones ran it. (See next page)

1930s - Mrs F Jones was Landlady of the Allenby, 15 St Nicholas Cliff in the 1930s

The photo below was taken in 1914 before her marriage. Her maiden name was Cody.

1930's – This appears to be a Wedding celebration with guests standing on the steps of No 15. Mrs F Jones is circled.

In the photo on the left Mrs Jones' appears in later years, seated in the centre. Her daughter is on the left and Mrs Jones' husband on the right.

57

The photo of this group was also taken on the steps of the No. 15 (The Allenby).
Left to right front row: Mr Jones, Mrs F Jones (centre), Mrs Jones' daughter. The daughter appears to be dressed in uniform.

1933 - Advert for Allenby

THE WESTBOROUGH BOARDING HOUSE
66 WESTBOROUGH

Near Railway Station. Central for both Bays. Good Catering our Speciality. Country Produce.
TERMS £2 2 0 PER WEEK.
N.B.—The Proprietress's aim is efficiency and is highly recommended throughout the British Isles. OPEN ALL THE YEAR
Mrs. C. HITCH, Proprietress.
Miss C. HITCH, Manageress.

THE ALLENBY
ST. NICHOLAS CLIFF
CENTRAL FOR ALL PARTS

Facing Grand Hotel. Overlooks South Bay and Main Entrance to Spa.
Noted for Homeliness and Excellent Catering. Electric throughout. Separate Tables.
Personal Supervision.
Special Terms for Early and Late Season also for Conferences.

Proprietress : Mrs. F. JONES

1930's - Aerial photograph of the Cliff

1933– Page from Scarborough Guide

THE WESTBOROUGH BOARDING HOUSE
66 WESTBOROUGH

Near Railway Station. Central for both Bays. Good Catering our Speciality. Country Produce.
TERMS £2 2 0 PER WEEK.
N.B.—The Proprietress's aim is efficiency and is highly recommended throughout the British Isles.   **OPEN ALL THE YEAR**

Mrs. C. HITCH, Proprietress.
Miss C. HITCH, Manageress.

THE ALLENBY
ST. NICHOLAS CLIFF
CENTRAL FOR ALL PARTS

Facing Grand Hotel. Overlooks South Bay and Main Entrance to Spa. Noted for Homeliness and Excellent Catering. Electric throughout. Separate Tables. Personal Supervision.
Special Terms for Early and Late Season also for Conferences.

Proprietress: Mrs. F. JONES

MARSHGATE
50 ABERDEEN WALK

Board Residence. Central for both Bays and all Amusements. Good Cooking. Small Tables. E.L. throughout. H. & C. Bath. Garage half a minute. Very highly recommended.
Moderate Terms and Special for Winter.
Write for Tariff.

Proprietress: Mrs. C. N. RIDSDALE

STANDEVEN'S
11 SANDSIDE (opposite Harbour and S. BAY)
Telephone 1205
BOARD RESIDENCE 8/6 and 9/- PER DAY
Bed and Breakfast Single 5/6 Double 10/-
Hot & Cold Water. Electric Light every bedroom
OUR GUARANTEE: Realising the uncertainty of receiving satisfaction when booking rooms unseen, and to remove this difficulty, we agree to allow any client to terminate his contract within 48 hours of arrival, should he not be satisfied, without any obligation other than paying for services already received.
RESTAURANT ADJOINING SEATING 250
Same Management

THORESBY
BOARDING HOUSE
53, QUEEN'S PARADE

Overlooking NORTH BAY
EXCELLENTLY SITUATED

All Bedrooms fitted with Hot & Cold Water. Electric Light throughout
Personal attention to ensure individual comfort
For Tariff, apply L. INGHAM

"LYNWODE"
15, ALBION ROAD
SOUTH CLIFF

Close to Esplanade, Spa, Bathing Pool, Tennis.

Highly recommended for catering and comfort

Separate Tables.   Terms moderate

Mrs. D. DYSON

THE KENSINGTON
PRIVATE HOTEL AND BOARDING HOUSE

Overlooking the South Bay and Sands, the Park and the beautiful Spa Grounds. The prettiest position in Scarborough. Five minutes from Station. Terms moderate. Balcony Bedrooms first floor. Central for everything. Modernized throughout. Hot and Cold Water in all Bedrooms and Electric Light.   'Phone 1120
ALDERSON'S - - Proprietors
CLIFF BRIDGE TERRACE
SCARBOROUGH

GILLSIDE
ST. MARTIN'S SQUARE, SOUTH CLIFF
Telephone 1389

Within two minutes of the Spa, Esplanade and Gardens. Electric Light throughout. Hot and Cold Water.   Separate Tables.

Season Terms from 9/6 per day
Reduced Terms out of Season
— Tariff on Application

Proprietress: Mrs. FREEMAN

Page Eighty-six

1937 - Advert for The Allenby

THE ALLENBY

PRIVATE HOTEL

ST. NICHOLAS CLIFF

CENTRAL FOR ALL PARTS

Facing Grand Hotel. Overlooks South Bay and Main Entrance to Spa.

Noted for Homeliness and Excellent Catering. Electric throughout.

HOT AND COLD WATER IN ALL BEDROOMS

Recently renovated with modern furnishings and decorations. Separate Tables.

TERMS

from 9/6 to 11/- per day

PERSONAL SUPERVISION

Special Terms for Early and Late Season.

Tel. 465. Proprietress: Mrs. F. JONES

Map G 7

1937 – Page from Scarborough Guide

BEDFORD PRIVATE HOTEL
THE CRESCENT

Charmingly situated in an ideal, central but quiet position. South aspect, facing Sea and Private Gardens. Two minutes from Spa, Medical Baths and the Sea. Hot and Cold Water and Gas Fires in Bedrooms. Spacious Dining Room, Lounge and Separate Writing Room.

Electric Light throughout. Open all the year round.

Renowned for Cuisine and Comfort.

INCLUSIVE TERMS from 3½ guineas to 5 guineas

Telephone 84   Proprietress: Mrs. E. STEVENSON

Map G 7

THE ALLENBY
PRIVATE HOTEL
ST. NICHOLAS CLIFF

CENTRAL FOR ALL PARTS

Facing Grand Hotel. Overlooks South Bay and Main Entrance to Spa.

Noted for Homeliness and Excellent Catering. Electric throughout.

HOT AND COLD WATER IN ALL BEDROOMS

Recently renovated with modern furnishings and decorations. Separate Tables.

TERMS
from 9/6 to 11/- per day

PERSONAL SUPERVISION
Special Terms for Early and Late Season.
Tel. 465.   Proprietress: Mrs. F. JONES

Map G 7

FAIRHOLME PRIVATE HOTEL
9, THE VALLEY

A delightful holiday home, pleasantly and conveniently situated in the Valley Gardens with level approach to the Sea and Spa. Spacious Winter Garden unique in the district, electric lighting. Table Tennis, etc., make "Fairholme" ideal for those who take HOLIDAYS EARLY AND LATE.

HOT AND COLD WATER ALL BEDROOMS
Excellent and generous catering. Late Dinner. Inclusive Terms from 9/- per day are decidedly reasonable. Tariff on application from the Proprietors: Mr. and Mrs. J. D. Field. Tel. No. 719

Map H 6

THE MILTON
ALMA SQUARE

Delightfully situated. Central for Sea, Spa and all Entertainments. Railway, Bus Stations and Garage 1 minute. Excellent and varied Cuisine with English Meat only. Fruit and Vegetables from our own Garden. Liberal Table and well-aired comfortable Beds. Electric Light throughout. Enlarged and re-decorated. Accommodation 50. Hot and Cold Running Water in Bedrooms. Moderate Terms, full board from 9/-. Bed and Breakfast from 6/-. Book early for single rooms to avoid disappointment. Tourists catered for. Headquarters of The British Motor Cycle Association. Private Car Park. Tariff on application.

Tel. 2081   Props.: Mr. and Misses BRADLEY   Grams: Milton Hotel, Scarbro'

Don't forget to write for *The Milton Special Holiday Folder*—See page 110

Map G 6

1938 – Page from Scarborough Guide for Riviera Hotel

at the Riviera
the whole of the South Bay is spread out before you!

SCARBOROUGH'S glorious South Bay on your doorstep! With its lovely, ever-changing seascape! With all its varied entertainment! Bathing, Dancing, Tennis, Theatres. Lazing in the sunshine... listening to music... living a happy, carefree life in the gayest of surroundings. Certainly the Riviera is at the very centre of things.

And a comfortable centre, too. Cosy bedrooms, each with Vi-spring mattresses and hot and cold running water, many with gas or electric fires. Comfortable lounges and a large recreation room. Charming dining-room, with the best of food to satisfy healthy Scarborough appetites.

Garage adjacent. Frequent bus service close at hand, serving two Golf Courses, North Bay, and glorious moors nearby. Shops just around the corner.

And personal service always. Every quiet comfort and convenience for a happier holiday. The Riviera is open all the year round—there's always a welcome for *you*, and a good time assured.

Riviera private hotel

★ **TARIFF.** *Inclusive Terms : Mid-July to Mid-September 11/6 to 15/6 per day.* Other periods 9/6 to 12/6 per day. The catering and management are under the personal supervision of Mr. and Mrs. R. H. Lund. Full illustrated tariff will be sent gladly on request.

ST. NICHOLAS CLIFF. Tel.: Scarborough 479

In 1939 - Number 15 became part of the Riviera as the advert in the Scarborough Guide describes it as "Newly enlarged. 20 more bedrooms added. Additional Lounge and Recreation Room". As far as could be ascertained the buildings were never connected internally, just accessed by staff at the doors at the back and front of the buildings.

1939 - Page from Scarborough Guide

RIVIERA PRIVATE HOTEL

Overlooking South Bay
Central for Everything
ONE MINUTE TO SPA
SANDS CLIFFS
TOWN & THEATRES
NEAR MEDICAL BATHS

OPEN ALL YEAR ROUND

Central for North and South Bays. Hot and Cold Running Water in all Bedrooms. New Furnishings and Decorations. Vi-Spring Mattresses on all Beds. Separate Tables. High-class Catering. Sea Views. Newly Enlarged. 20 more Bedrooms added. Additional Lounge and Recreation Room. 5 Lounges. Accommodation 100.

The Food and Cooking in this Hotel is a special feature combined with first-class service
Inclusive Terms : Mid-July—Mid-September 10/6—14/6 per day ; other periods 9/6—12/6 per day
Garage adjacent   Electric Light throughout   No Restrictions   Personal Supervision
Tariff on Request   Telephone 479   Mr. and Mrs. R. H. LUND

Map G. 7

THE REGENT — BOARDING ESTABLISHMENT

29, NEWBOROUGH

Tel. 2460

SITUATED IN THE MAIN STREET
DEFINITELY CENTRAL FOR EVERYWHERE
3 MINS. SEA, SPA, GARDENS
LARGE DINING ROOM   SEPARATE TABLES
GOOD SERVICE   SPLENDID VARIETY OF WELL-COOKED MEALS
COMFORTABLE LOUNGE

OPEN ALL THE YEAR ROUND

INCLUSIVE TERMS 8/- PER DAY
MAY, JUNE AND SEPT., 45/- WEEKLY

GARAGE NEARBY   Write for Tariff : Mrs. M. G. JONES, Proprietress

Map F. 7

Index in each advertisement gives position on Map.   Page 79

1940 – Advert Riviera

RIVIERA PRIVATE HOTEL
CENTRAL FOR NORTH AND SOUTH BAYS.

Hot and Cold running Water in all Bedrooms.

Vi-Spring Mattresses on all beds

Five Lounges

Accommodation 100

The Food and Cooking in this Hotel is a Special Feature combined with First Class service, and will be maintained.

COME AND SEE! Why not a week or two with NO RATIONING worries? Garage adjacent. Electric light throughout. No restrictions. Personal Supervision. Terms Moderate. Telephone 479

Mr. and Mrs. R. H. LUND.   ST. NICHOLAS CLIFF   Map G. 7

1940 – In **Scarborough Guide** number 15 was still part of the Riviera.

The advert picture of 1940 highlights 15 visually as part of the Riviera.

Chapter 8 - 1940 - 1972

1940 – Whole page Scarborough Guide

Mayfair PRIVATE HOTEL

Esplanade

- OVERLOOKING THE WHOLE OF THE SOUTH BAY
- IN THE CENTRE OF THE ESPLANADE
- TWO MINUTES' WALK ON THE LEVEL FROM THE SPA LIFT

This is the Private Hotel of Distinction for those discriminating people who appreciate Comfort in its highest sense—perfectly cooked Meals and generous Catering combined with a cheerful and friendly atmosphere

PASSENGER LIFT

Inclusive Terms to suit War-reduced Incomes

Telephone No. 53.
Telegrams: "Mayfair, Esplanade, Scarborough."

Proprietress: Miss A. J. C. MACKENZIE

Map I. 7

RIVIERA PRIVATE HOTEL
CENTRAL FOR NORTH AND SOUTH BAYS.

Hot and Cold running Water in all Bedrooms.

Vi-Spring Mattresses on all beds

Five Lounges

Accommodation 100

The Food and Cooking in this Hotel is a Special Feature combined with First Class service, and will be maintained.

COME AND SEE! Why not a week or two with NO RATIONING worries? Garage adjacent. Electric light throughout. No restrictions. Personal Supervision. Terms Moderate. Telephone 479.

Mr. and Mrs. R. H. LUND. ST. NICHOLAS CLIFF

Map G. 7

Code Index in each advertisement gives position on Map.

Page 63

Through the remaining Second World War years number 15 came in use for the Masonic Hall.

Lighting Restrictions

The Management have taken all reasonable precautions for the darkening of windows, and any persons showing a light do so at their own risk and are liable to Police prosecution

1947 -

1949 – On 4th June, number 15 was auctioned for Sale.

It was purchased by Ideal Estates (Doncaster) Limited for the sum of £5,000. Frank Haslam was a Director of Ideal Estates.

The St Nicholas Hotel ran it for the next three years.

1952 - Post card of the Stewart Hotel

1952 - Number 15 was sold to Mr. C. W. Poskitt and Mrs. J. Poskitt on the 17th April, for the sum of £5,700. They named it the Stewart Hotel and were experienced in the trade, moving from their family hotel, Brunswick Lodge Hotel, Brunswick Terrace. This is where the Brunswick Pavilion Shopping Centre is nowadays.

Mr. Clifford Poskitt was an apprenticed trained painter and decorator and he painted a contour map of Scarborough, which is partly shown on the 1971 photograph of the Reception. Clifford was a relative of Bertie Whitaker, who used to have the Grand Restaurant near the Roller Skating

Rink. These were situated directly beneath the Grand Hotel on the sea front, shown on the aerial photograph of the **1930's**.
Bertie Whitaker lived for a time at the Chalet over Spa Bridge.

1956 - Watercolour painted by Pat Faust, showing the Toll Gate on the Spa Bridge

1959 Scarborough Guide advert for Stewart Hotel

STEWART†   15 St. Nicholas Cliff (C)

Inclusive Terms:

From 25/- to 27/- per day. Children according to age. Reduced terms out of season.

These terms include bed, breakfast, dinner and high tea. Evening refreshments.

Modern Private Hotel beautifully situated facing the sea, spring interior beds, pleasant lounge. Situation for all Conferences is ideal. Near to Spa, gardens, beach, cinemas and G.P.O. Garages adjoining. Good Yorkshire cooking. Personal supervision.

Telephone: 1095   Proprietors: Mr. & Mrs. C. W. Poskitt

Map G.7

1959 – Page from Scarborough Guide

SEA CREST†   31/32/33 Blenheim Terrace (N)

Inclusive Terms:
Mid-June to mid-Sept. 19/6 per day, mid-Sept. to mid-June 17/6 per day. Reduction for children.

Sea front Private Hotel. Every comfort and consideration. 42 bedrooms all h. & c. water and interior sprung beds. Cosy lounge with 21 inch television and library. Separate tables. Owners' personal supervision.

Telephone: 3851   Proprietors: Mr. & Mrs. C. Burgess   Map E.7

SOUTHDOWN†   4 Cliff Bridge Terrace (C)

Inclusive Terms:
Per day, single 22/6 to 27/6. These terms include bed, breakfast, lunch, dinner and evening refreshments.

Modern Private Hotel, most convenient and unrivalled position on St. Nicholas Cliff, the heart of Scarborough, facing due South. Overlooking sea, Spa and adjacent to beach, lift, the Medical Baths, Woodend gardens and principal shopping centre. Conference area. H. & c., interior sprung beds. Free parking or large garage adjoining.

Telephone: 283   Proprietors: J. & G. Brown   Map G.7

STEWART†   15 St. Nicholas Cliff (C)

Inclusive Terms:
From 25/- to 27/- per day. Children according to age. Reduced terms out of season.
These terms include bed, breakfast, dinner and high tea. Evening refreshments.

Modern Private Hotel beautifully situated facing the sea, spring interior beds, pleasant lounge. Situation for all Conferences is ideal. Near to Spa, gardens, beach, cinemas and G.P.O. Garages adjoining. Good Yorkshire cooking. Personal supervision.

Telephone: 1095   Proprietors: Mr. & Mrs. C. W. Poskitt   Map G.7

SUNNY LEIGH†   46 Devonshire Drive (N)

Inclusive Terms:
Per day, 18/6 to 20/-. Bed and breakfast 12/6. Reduced terms early and late season. These terms include bed, breakfast, dinner, high tea and light supper.

Modern Guest House situated overlooking Peasholm Park, near Open Air Theatre, Floral Hall, and cricket ground, etc. Ground floor lounge and dining room. All bedrooms h. & c. water and spring interiors. All on two floors. Free car space. Open all year round.

Telephone: 962   Proprietress: Mrs. W. G. Bottomley   Map E.5

SUSSEX†   West Street (S)

Inclusive Terms:
Per day, single from 20/- to 25/- according to room and season.
These terms include bed, breakfast, lunch, dinner and light supper.

Select Private Hotel. 2 mins. Spa, Esplanade, Italian and rose gardens and tennis. Near South Bay bathing pool and beach. H. & c. water all bedrooms and interior sprung mattresses. Separate tables, lounge. Within easy reach town centre. Garages adjacent. First class food, service and accommodation. Personal supervision. *A small Hotel with a large reputation.*

Telephone: 886   Proprietors: Mr. & Mrs. W. J. Hunter.   Map I.7

Photos of the Poskitts

1971 – In December Mr. Clifford Poskitt sold the Stewart Hotel to Mr. Don Pummell for the sum of £15,500.

Don Pummell was an apprenticed trained painter and decorator with Rowntrees, moving from a small Guest House, The Argo Hotel, 134 North Marine Road. He also gained City and Guilds in Catering. Don lived in Canada for 3 years in the 1950's.

Don was always the worker and had three jobs in Canada to acquire finance for buying his own property. He then came back for his love of Scarborough.

1971 - Photograph of Reception of the Stewart Hotel

1972 - Photograph of Don Pummell in the back yard of The Stewart Hotel after moving in

The first summer season was 1972 and money was in short supply after the purchase, so we had to "make do and mend". Don decorated the lounge, entrance and dining room - all the bedrooms and enormous yet beautiful cantilevered staircase would have to wait. (The staircase would have been built so wide, to accommodate for the access of cabin trunks and other large luggage of its visitors, in the late 18th Century of a Lodging House.) The bedroom landings were enormous too and each the size of a bedroom.

There were 3 bathrooms and one toilet to service the 19 visitor bedrooms. We had three small rooms and a bathroom behind the Reception. At least each visitor bedroom had a wash hand basin. I remember, the old boiler struggled heating the water and it took hours to recover after a peak time. When we had 45 guests staying in the school holidays, we had to put a sign up requesting visitors to have a bath after dinner - otherwise we ran out of hot water for washing up!

Generally, we offered dinner, bed and breakfast. There was a choice of menu at Breakfast, and Dinner consisted of soup and homemade bread rolls, set main course and a choice of dessert displayed on the centre table.

For certain groups of people, it was full board. The Benelux Festival, which was in June, was one of those group times. Don arranged with the Town Hall to charge special lower rates for full board to take a Dutch Band and it was very entertaining for us too. Christmas time was another of those full board times.

We offered a "3 day Christmas Package" with in house entertainment (games of Beetle, Bingo, various Quiz, and Horse Racing) and a trip to a local hunt on Boxing Day. In later years, we took them to a Pantomime at the Spa and encouraged a fancy dress dinner competition i.e. we had to set a good example and dress up too. Most visitors made their costumes and some were wonderful; the Green Hulk and one man as ballet dancer were quite spectacular.

After the first summer, Don was able to evaluate what was needed. The work commenced on making a bar on ground floor level in the **Autumn of 1972**. *Pat Tovell, was a joiner friend, and assisted to make the ugly ground floor bedroom into a welcoming panelled bar with the addition of mirrors from the old Pavilion Hotel (which was shortly to be demolished). When out of school holidays, we usually had up 30 people a week staying between June and until the end of September. However, in the school holidays the number soared up to 48 at the most. It was like having a school some weeks! The children made friends! We charged a very low rate for children. Don said, " we take children to get their parents!" It was a relief for me when September came - less workload, and less mess. I was Front of House (Reception, Waitress, Housekeeper and Cleaner); Don was Cook and Maintenance, as well as new ideas and Administrator.*

Chapter 9 1972 - 1981

1972 – Page from Scarborough Guide

*SEAVIEW HOTEL ★   Prince of Wales Terrace (S)

Full Board Terms from £2·50 a day. Reductions Early and Late seasons. Write or 'phone for Colour Brochure and sample Menu.

Tel: 0723 61177   Map I.7

"STOP HERE"
THE SMALL HOTEL WITH BIG IDEAS

* We are proud of our Traditional English Breakfast with a choice of 10 different dishes every day!
* There is a choice of food at every meal, personally cooked by the Proprietor.
* Our 'Little Bar' is open until midnight (Residential Licence) and we offer Late Night Snacks.
* Taste our Dinner Wine FREE before you buy and if it is your Honeymoon, FREE Champagne!
* Our Lounge and Front Bedrooms all have a sea view.
* We are situated opposite beautiful gardens, only 120 yards from the Esplanade and Lift to SPA, BEACH and POOL etc.. Ideal for Holidays. Conference delegates especially welcome.

Resident Proprietors: Dawn and Jerry Harrow.

SEFTON ★   (S)
18 Prince of Wales Terr.

Terms: From £2·10 to £2·30 per day. These terms include Bath, Bed, Breakfast, Lunch and Dinner. Bed, Breakfast and Dinner from £1·90. Bed and Breakfast from £1·60. The owners of THE SEFTON assure you of a warm welcome. LARGE BEDROOMS make it ideal for family holidays. TWO MINUTES to SPA LIFT makes it ideal for CONFERENCE DELEGATES. Gas or electric fires in most rooms. LIFT TO ALL FLOORS. Personal service and GOOD FOOD ASSURED.

Proprietors:
Mr. & Mrs. Harold Lee

Telephone: 2310 (STD 0723)

Map I.7

SOUTHLANDS HOTEL
SOUTH CLIFF

Terms: Per day, season from £3·00. Reduced terms in the Annex. Winter from £2·50. Winter residential terms on application. These terms include Bed, Breakfast Lunch and Dinner. Afternoon Teas served on request. This first-class Hotel (conditional licence) is open all the year round. 70 well furnished bedrooms all with central heating, 12 with private bathrooms. Excellent public rooms with open fires. Large Dining Room, modern attractive Cocktail Bar. Television Room, Games Room. Lift to all floors. Near Spa Gardens and Bathing Pool and within easy reach of tennis and golf clubs. Sunny gardens. Private car park.

Illustrated brochure on request

Map I.7 (S) ★   *Telephone: Scarborough 61447*

STEWART HOTEL   ★ 15 St. Nicholas Cliff

★ Good English Food.
★ Television Lounge.
★ In the heart of Conference Area.
★ Personal Supervision.
★ Special Terms, early and late season.
★ Car Park.
★ No Service Charge.
★ Overlooking South Bay.
★ Near Lifts for South Bay.
★ Close to Shopping Centre.
★ Terms: £2·00 to £3·00 per day, according to position of room and season. These terms are for Bed, Breakfast and Evening Dinner.

Proprietor: D. Pummell

Telephone: 61095 or 61199

Map G.7

SYLVANA PRIVATE HOTEL ★ 41 Grosvenor Road (S)

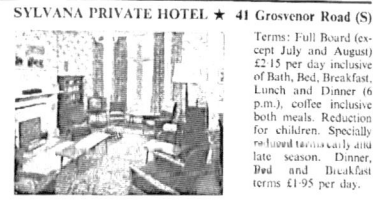

Terms: Full Board (except July and August) £2·15 per day inclusive of Bath, Bed, Breakfast, Lunch and Dinner (6 p.m.), coffee inclusive both meals. Reduction for children. Specially reduced terms early and late season. Dinner, Bed and Breakfast terms £1·95 per day.

The Sylvana is a well appointed Private Hotel, highly recommended, situated between Grosvenor Road and Valley Road. Within a few minutes walk of the Spa, sea front and Italian Gardens. Convenient for Scarborough's many amenities, theatres, conference halls and within easy reach of main shopping centre. Spacious dining room with separate tables. The proprietress ensures complete satisfaction. Noted for its homely atmosphere and the quality, quantity and variety of food served, including continental dishes if requested. All bedrooms h. & c., spring interior mattresses, razor points, fitted carpets, central or electric heating, TV lounge, library. Free parking.

Proprietress: Mrs. H. Kramer, 41 Grosvenor Road

Telephone: 60779   Map H.6

1973

In 1973 a brief encounter with a Government Official (he just rang the door bell), searching for potential buildings to 'List' allowed number 15 to be awarded Grade II Listed Building Status.

Details of Listed Building 1973

Circa 1770 – 1780, House in terrace, 4 storeys painted brick with basement. Wood triglyph frieze and eaves cornice. 3 square windows to 3rd floor, late casements from 2nd floor on left hand broad canted wood bay, mid 19th Century, pilasters dividing lights on each floor with frieze and cornice over. Tall recessed sashes to right above entrance that on 2nd floor retaining glazing bars. Door of 6 field panels semi circular fan light. Good door case of engaged composit, Corinthian columns, broken entablative with urn reliefs to front, open dentil pediment. Area railings carried up steps to door have turned iron rails and finialed standard.

Interior has full height rectangular stairwell, top light with cantilevered open string staircase with slender turned banisters swept continuous moulded hand rail. Ground floor front room has paneled dado and marble fireplace surround flanked by fluted pilasters. Good iron carved basket grate with fluting.

1974 - Photograph

1975 - *After recovering from the expense of the Fire Precautions Act – 1972, and having 3 busy seasons, Don was able to invest some money in the building. So a plan of improvements was drawn up which began again in 1976.*

1976 - *Six rooms were made en-suite, Ray Shannon being the plumber and this took the pressure off the queues for* the 3 bathrooms. Other bedrooms were only decorated on the lower 3 floors.

The top floor of bedrooms were attic type rooms. Three rooms were let to visitors with proper level windows, and one room was for the "live in" girls. This room had a small high window, mainly to let in a little natural light. (I suspect these were always the servants' rooms in the building's early years.) If there was a repair to be done on the Georgian Sky Light, Don had to crawl through this small window and balance on the Rosemary tiled roof. The Sky Light let in borrowed light all down the staircase to ground floor level. Thus, it was quite a height to fall should this Georgian window deteriorate even more. We never told visitors, but there was a passage under the eaves, which went all around the top floor from room to room, the entrance being through a small door in each room. To access this passage it was necessary to crawl. To my knowledge no one ever took advantage of this facility! Our price structure reflected the poorer quality rooms on the top floor: 4th floor of bedrooms, at £1.50 per day for Dinner, Bed and Breakfast in contrast to the lower rooms front £2.10 per day and back rooms £2.00 per day. There was a perk to the top floor visitor rooms – the views were beautiful. Thinking about all these factors, Don set in process in **1976** Plans to re-build this floor.

1976 - Permission was granted for Listed Building Consent to rebuild the top floor. Work by Major Builders commenced in winter, so it would be completed for the **1977 Season.**

Whilst demolishing the top floor, down to floorboard level, Don found, hidden behind a partition wall, an old folded letter dated 1750. He carefully opened it realizing it may be of some *interest. It was taken to the Museum for examination. Basically, it was addressed to certain persons for selling drinks without a license, and they had to appear at a court hearing at the sign of the Crooked Billet. An article was put in the local newspaper but we never found where the Crooked Billet was situated.*

1977 - Letter found, dated 1750

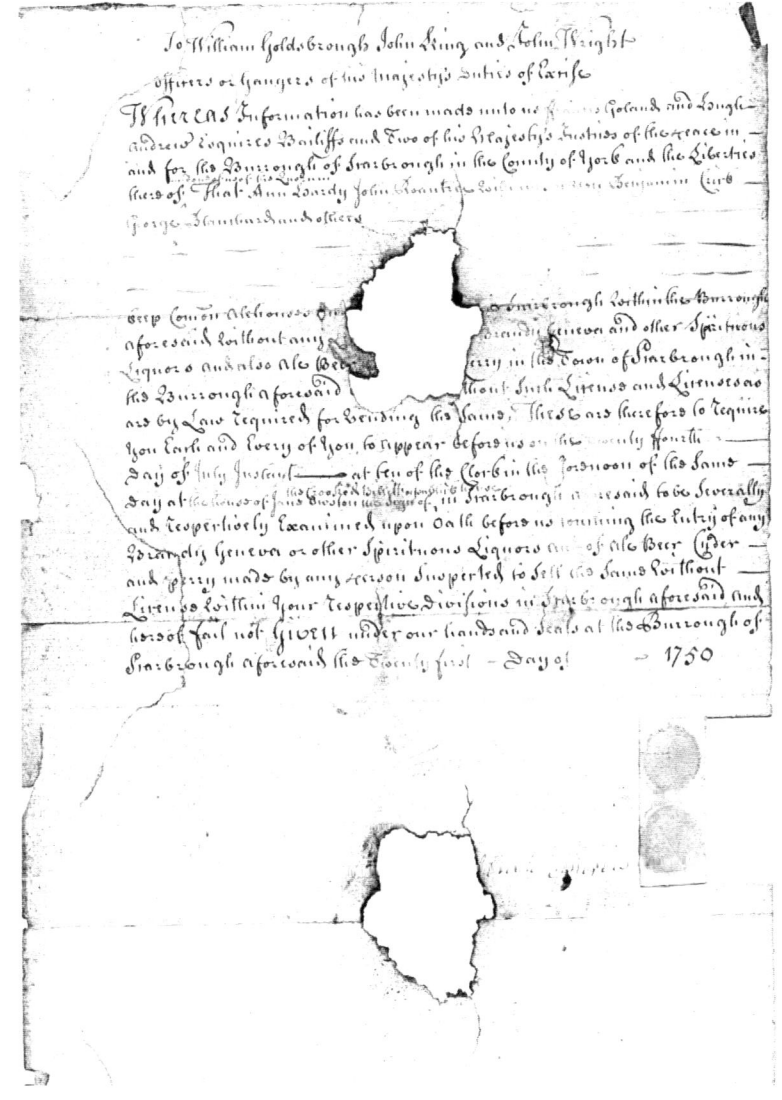

1977 – Transcript of 1750 Letter

Translation of 1750 letter found behind a partition wall, on the top floor of the Stewart Hotel in 1977, when it was being re-built.

> To William Goldsborough, John King, and John Wright Officers or Gangers of his Majesty's Duties of Excise.
>
> Whereas information has been made unto us Francis Goland and Hugh Andrew and said Esquires, Bailiffs and two of his Majesty's Justices of the peace in and for the Borough of Scarborough in the County of York and the Liberties thereof that Ann Bardy, John Rowntree and William Jackson, Benjamin Kirb, George Blanchard and others _ _ _ _ _ _ _ _ _ _
> _
> _
> Keep common alehouses …………… in Scarborough with in the Borough aforesaid without any……………… brandy, Geneva and other spirituous Liquors and also ale, beer ……… (pe)rry in this town of Scarborough in the Borough aforesaid …………. (wi)thout such License and Licenses as are by Law required for brewing the same. These are therefore to require you each and every of you to appear before us on the twenty fourth day of July Instant ------ at ten of the clock in the forenoon of the same day at the house of Jane Owston, the sign of the Crooked Billet a public house in Scarborough aforesaid to be severely and respectively examined upon oath before us ….. hing the entry of any brandy, geneva or spirituous liquors and of ale, beer; cider and perry made by any reason suspected to sell the same without license within your respective divisions in Scarborough aforesaid and loss of fail not given under our hands and seats at the Borough of Scarborough aforesaid this twenty first day of July 1750
>
> (signed by)   ◯ seals
>
> *Francis Goland* (senior Bailiff equivalent to Mayor)   ◯
>
> *Hugh Andrew* (junior Bailiff equivalent to Deputy Mayor

1977 – 3 Photos of building work in process.

Below: Don decorating Room 9

1977 - Aerial Photograph of the Cliff

1978 – Stewart Hotel Guide Advert.

STEWART HOTEL

**ST. NICHOLAS CLIFF
YO11 2ES**

Proprietor: **D. Pummell**

Telephone: (STD 0723) 61095

TERMS:
Room with Breakfast and Evening Dinner from £5·00 per day per person.

Reduced terms for children sharing parents' bedroom.

Tea tray and electric kettle in all rooms.

Rooms with private toilet and shower are available.

SITUATED IN AN IDEAL POSITION OVERLOOKING THE SOUTH BAY AND CLOSE TO THE SHOPPING CENTRE.

Bar

Lounge

- Sea view from the lounge and front bedrooms
- Residents' Bar
- Good food is our speciality
- Two public car parks nearby

WE LOOK FORWARD TO MEETING YOU

Map G.7 (C)★*

1978 Scarborough Guide page

STEWART HOTEL

ST. NICHOLAS CLIFF YO11 2ES
Proprietor: **D. Pummell**
Telephone: (STD 0723) 61095

TERMS:
Room with Breakfast and Evening Dinner from £5·00 per day per person.

Reduced terms for children sharing parents' bedroom.

Tea tray and electric kettle in all rooms.

Rooms with private toilet and shower are available.

SITUATED IN AN IDEAL POSITION OVERLOOKING THE SOUTH BAY AND CLOSE TO THE SHOPPING CENTRE.

- Sea view from the lounge and front bedrooms
- Residents' Bar
- Good food is our speciality
- Two public car parks nearby

WE LOOK FORWARD TO MEETING YOU

Map G.7 (C)★*

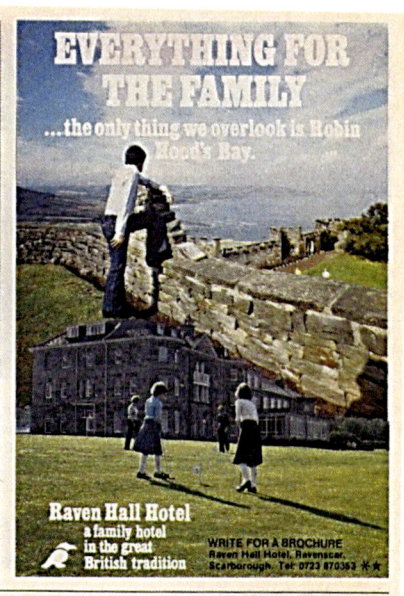

Bar
Lounge

EVERYTHING FOR THE FAMILY

...the only thing we overlook is Robin Hood's Bay.

Raven Hall Hotel
a family hotel in the great British tradition

WRITE FOR A BROCHURE
Raven Hall Hotel, Ravenscar, Scarborough. Tel: 0723 870353 ★★

Map G.6 (C)★*

BOSTON HOTEL
NORTH BAY, SCARBOROUGH, YO12 7HF

- A Private Hotel with one of the most commanding positions of the whole North Bay
- Lift to all floors
- Central for all attractions and town amenities
- 75 per cent of our bedrooms have sea views
- Two comfortable lounges—one with colour TV
- Personal supervision of the proprietors ensures comfort and high standard in catering
- Parties welcome
- All Fire Precautions completed

Terms: From £5·50 per day., Bed, Breakfast, Dinner and Light Supper. Reduced terms for children sharing with 2 adults.

Illustrated Brochure and Tariff on request S.A.E. please

Resident Proprietors:
Mr. and Mrs. J. W. Gourlay
Telephone: Reception (0723) 60296
Guests (0723) 62226

Map E.7 (N)★

VIEW FROM HOTEL

ATTENBOROUGH HOTEL
ALBEMARLE CRESCENT, YO11 1XX

- Charmingly situated Hotel overlooking gardens, central for both bays and amusements
- 43 bedrooms, all with H. & C., razor sockets and bedlights
- Renowned for excellent food and service, all personally supervised by resident proprietors
- Licensed lounge bar
- 2 comfortable lounges, one with colour TV
- Parking adjacent

TERMS:
Bed and Breakfast from £3·50
Dinner, Bed and Breakfast from £4·50
Evening Refreshments available
Proprietors: Mr. and Mrs. F. Hillier
Telephone: (0723) 60857 or (0723) 862191. Guests 73125

65

85

1981 - Christmas Norwegian cold table

Chapter 10 1982 - 2000

1982 - Scarborough Guide Advert showing the Bar (Note the changed telephone number. See page 89)

STEWART HOTEL

15 ST NICHOLAS CLIFF
Telephone
0723 61098̶5̶

Proprietor: D. Pummell
Situated in an ideal position overlooking the South Bay and close to the beach and shopping centre.

Tea tray with electric kettle in all rooms. Rooms with private shower, toilet, radio and television are available. Good food is an important part of a holiday. We make every effort to make sure you get good food.

Terms: From £7.00 per day per person Bed & Breakfast plus V.A.T. Reduced terms for children, sharing their parents' bedroom. Full English Breakfast. Evening Dinner.

Map G.7 (C)★*

1982 Scarborough Guide page

SCARBOROUGH Evening News

TUESDAY 16 FEBRUARY 1982

No. 30,195
10 Pence

General 63631
Tele-Ads 75533

5 x 47,000 EQUALS — WRITER'S CRAMP!

It was just a tiny slip in the Scarborough holiday accommodation guide. But the figure six that should have been a five will be forever etched on local hotelier Don Pummell's memory.

He, his wife, and their waitress are just recovering from a two-week stint altering about 47,000 guides by hand.

The slip appeared in the phone number for Mr Pummell's hotel, the Stewart Hotel, St Nicholas Cliff, in the newly published Scarborough accommodation guide.

Instead of 61095, it read 61096 — the number of a housewife in Green Lane. Mr Pummell discovered what had happened when an old customer rang him. Then he set off hot-foot for the Spa Ocean Room with his wife, Connie, and their waitress, Margaret Milam, to alter the copies that were stored there.

"The booklet had been out about two weeks before we realised that no-one was ringing," said Mr Pummell, who had had some new art-work done for this year's guide. "I hope the damage has been rectified by us crossing out the old number and putting in the right one."

At Green Lane, meanwhile, Mrs Jessie Webb has been taking dozens of calls inquiring about accommodation. "It's no trouble," she said. "We just keep saying that there's been an error and give them the correct number."

Scarborough Council's publicity officer, Mr Derrick Hagerston, said that one of the Council's checkers had spotted the wrong number, which had been put or the advertisement by mistake by the person who had done the art-work for Mr Pummell.

When the proof came back the number was still wrong and a white panel in the advert was missing. Both things were included in a list of corrections that went back to the printers, but only one was corrected. "It was a combination of things," he added.

So far, 32,562 copies of the Scarborough accommodation guide have gone out from a total print of 90,000. Mr Hagerston said that those which Mr Pummell had not corrected by hand would carry an erratum slip.

● MR. PUMMELL.

1983 - Photograph of the buildings 14 and 15.

Don's Butter carving

1986 - Connie and Don in the Dining Room

1986 - Photograph of the lounge

1989 - Christmas Fancy Dress

1990 - The Pummell family in the Lounge of the Stewart Hotel

1993 - Photograph of the Cliff.
This was the Bi-Centenary year for 14 and 15.

1993 - West side of the Cliff.

This was also the year of the disaster when the Holbeck Hall Hotel collapsed, but no lives were lost.

1993 - Photos of Don and Connie – Bi-Centenary Year

The 1990's - *were a struggle economically for most people: the Recession. We still managed to invest and improve the Stewart Hotel, making the remainder of the bedrooms en suites.*

Our daughters, Rachel and Sally, always regarded The Stewart as the family home, and loved living there with all the visitors and their children, but decided our working way of life was not for them and both went into the Teaching Profession, an equally hard job as it turned out!

1997 - Views from the top floor

*The bar was no longer producing sufficient income by **1999**, therefore Don changed it to a bedroom again. This room and extended area to the office was the original Dining Room in 1793. The dumbwaiter from the kitchen was positioned in the small office area behind the Reception desk.*

The borrowed light windows on the 1st floor of bedrooms had to be boxed in with plasterboard in the Fire Precautions Act 1972. The staircase also had to be boxed in with wired glass and self-closing doors.

2000 - Advert

STEWART HOTEL

15 St Nicholas Cliff, Scarborough, YO11 2ES
Tel: (01723) 361095 Fax: (01723) 350442
E-mail: don.pummell@onyxnet.co.uk

Enjoy the ambience and situation of this Grade II Listed Georgian Hotel, built 1793, appealing for pleasure or business. Mini Breaks.

Open all year. www.s-h-a.dircon.co.uk/

No. of bedrooms: 14.

Daily B&B p.per.
From £25

Proprietor:
D Pummell

2000 – Scarborough Guide page

SCARBOROUGH — HOTELS

THE SOUTHLANDS HOTEL
West Street, South Cliff, Scarborough, YO11 2QW
Tel: (01723) 361461 Fax: (01723) 376035

The Southlands Hotel on beautiful South Cliff, Scarborough. Called the home of hospitality by our regular guests. All 58 comfortable rooms have en-suite facilities, telephone, colour TV, tea/coffee etc. Lift to all floors. Large free adjacent car park. Limited disabled access. Excellent five course choice menu and childrens' menu. Ballroom with entertainment three times a week. Well stocked bar and wine cellar. Quiet non-smoking lounge. The Southlands is a spacious hotel, light and airey, offering a truly warm welcome to everyone. Please call today and ask for Tracy, Debbie or Nikky. Thank you.

No. of bedrooms: 58.

Daily B&B p.per. From £25.
Daily BB&EM p.per. From £34

Proprietors:
Epworth Hotels

WILLOW DENE HOTEL
110 Columbus Ravine, Scarborough, YO12 7QZ Tel: (01723) 365173

Prime position, near all attractions. Over 25 years experience offering excellent value. Good, varied menu. All rooms en-suite with TV's and teamaking. Five course dinner. Separate tables. Car park. Children half price. Low season including dinner three day break £59, four day £75. Senior citizens from £110 weekly. Highly recommended.

No. of bedrooms: 10.

Daily B&B p.per. From £16.
Daily BB&EM p.per. From £21

Proprietors:
Mr R W & Mrs E F Briggs

WEYDALE HOTEL
Weydale Avenue, Scarborough, YO12 6BA
Tel: (01723) 373393 Fax: (01723) 355734 E-mail: weydale.hotel@btinternet.com

Highly recommended, superbly located. All en-suite. Detached, licensed. North Bay view hotel renowned for warm Yorkshire welcome! The cosy rooms are well equipped and have comfortable, quality orthopaedic beds! Offering generous portions of traditional Yorkshire fayre, freshly prepared on the premises, including the already famous "Big Breakfast"! Family owned and managed.

No. of bedrooms: 24.

Daily B&B p.per. From £20
Daily BB&EM p.per. From £27

Proprietors: David & Ruth Frank

STEWART HOTEL
15 St Nicholas Cliff, Scarborough, YO11 2ES
Tel: (01723) 361095 Fax: (01723) 350442
E-mail: don.pummell@onyxnet.co.uk

Enjoy the ambience and situation of this Grade I Listed Georgian Hotel, built 1793, appealing for pleasure or business. Mini Breaks.
Open all year. www.s-h-a.dircon.co.uk/
No. of bedrooms: 14.

Daily B&B p.per.
From £25

Proprietor:
D Pummell

ARLINGTON HOTEL
42 West Street, South Cliff, Scarborough, YO11 2QP Tel: (01723) 503600

Highly recommended licensed hotel, with friendly atmosphere. All rooms (including two family) en-suite and appointed to a very high standard including TV, teasmaid, clock-radio, hairdryer, c/h. Near Spa and gardens. Ideal for conference delegates. Excellent cuisine with choice of menu in summer. Easy parking/garage. Weekly reductions. Colour brochure available.

No. of bedrooms: 10.

Daily B&B p.per. From £19.
Daily BB&EM p.per. From £27

Proprietors:
Carol Hatje, Alex Anderson

KERRY LEE (100% NON-SMOKING) HOTEL
60 Trafalgar Square, Scarborough, YO12 7PY
Tel: (01723) 363845   Colin & Jackie Charles

Family run guest house close to all attractions. TV, tea/coffee all rooms. Menu choice. Own keys. Open all year. Pets welcome. Non smoking throughout. No. of bedrooms: 8

Daily B&B p.per. From £12.
Daily BB&EM p.per. From £16

MOUNTVIEW PRIVATE HOTEL (Non Smoking)
32 West Street, South Cliff, Scarborough, YO11 2QP
Tel: (01723) 500608 Fax: (01723) 501385
www.mountview-hotel.co.uk e-mail: stay@mountview-hotel.co.uk

Lovely Victorian private hotel, situated close to Esplanade, Spa, gardens. Ideal for conference delegates, holidaymakers. Excellent reputation for English and vegetarian cuisine. Well appointed en-suite bedrooms, including ground floor. All with TV, radio alarm, hairdryer, beverage trays, central heating. Mid/part week bookings. Always open – easy parking. Family run. Brochure available.

No. of bedrooms: 7.

Daily B&B p.per. From £19.
Daily BB&EM p.per. From £27

Proprietors:
Derek & Sandy Stephenson

ADMIRAL HOTEL
13 West Square, Scarborough, YO11 1TW
Tel/Fax: (01723) 375084

- Ideally situated in town centre, directly opposite railway station, yards from theatre.
- Perfect for couples
- Ensuite rooms tastefully appointed with colour television, teamaking facilities and c.h.
- Late breakfasts/breakfasts in bed available, also room only if required (please ring for rates)
- Well recommended • Open all year

No. of bedrooms: 7

Daily B&B p.per. From £15.

Proprietors: Dave & Julie Driscoll

2000 - Don Pummell sold the Stewart Hotel in July to Barbara Ann Keen for £190,000

*The **original Dining room** was at the back of the building on the ground floor up to about 1952. Sometime between 1952 and 1971 this area was made into number 1 bedroom and private rooms.*

In 1972 the bar was made from number 1 bedroom, then when this bar was closed in 1999 it was made back into a bedroom.

*The **Dining room from the 1952 to 2005**, when this was written, was in the lower ground floor/basement, positioned where the Housekeeper's Room or Servants Hall used to be in the buildings early years.*

*The **Kitchen** is in the same position it has always been. But any Coach House, Stables and Wash House have long since been demolished in the back yard area.*

There are signs in the building work, that there was once a front entrance below stairs for the servants, both at number 14 and 15. These were changed many years ago. In number 15 there are still the flagstones down for this entrance inside.

The street level main front entrance used to lead straight through to the back yard, as shown by the parallel arches near to ceiling height. This would have been an entrance for the gentry.

Because these buildings were built as a Lodging Houses there are no back stairs for servants, as there would have been if houses were for private use for residing Gentlemen.

Needless to say the charming Lounge on the ground floor at the front of the building of number 15, will always be enhanced by the hypnotic view of the sea and the coastline towards Filey.

*In the midst of all this work, we bought some old farm labourers' cottages at Flixton in **1982**. It was with the vision to build a small hotel with purpose built en-suites, adjoining home and a car park. After satisfying the needs of legislation, work commenced in **1983**. So our working days adjusted to run the Stewart in conjunction with the building project. Don's day consisted of hotel Breakfast service then dashing off to Flixton for the various jobs associated with building a small hotel. He mainly laboured and observed work in progress. Often he was "the Go For!" for the tradesmen to keep work moving on. He came home to finish the hotel Dinner service and after his own meal, ran the bar until about 11.00 pm. My day adjusted around Don's new schedule. Consequently, it began with Breakfast service, moving on to the cleaning routine, servicing visitors' bedrooms and general house cleaning. Sandwiched between was my lunch, shopping, reception work and family life. At about 4.00 pm, I began the "en place" for hotel Dinner, this was intermingled with reception bells, phone calls and family. Our youngest daughter, Sally, was born in the early years of this project. My Mother lived with us for many years, which probably saved my sanity.*

***The 1980's** were this routine of the Stewart and project building work. The 1990's hit us like a sledgehammer, business down, no incoming profit to feed the project. We were in limbo. Don used to go to the Flixton project but only do work which cost nothing - work on the land mainly. He decided to go out on the "Tools" again and started painting and decorating for a cash flow. The Bank was doing a dance and sending letters like confetti for a return on some of their money!*
Then Don hit on the idea of re-furbishing the Stewart ready for sale! Completing the remainder of the en-

suites and decorating again and I cleaned! What a lot of sawdust and plaster dust! I made new curtains again (20 pairs), with a lovely bright satin cotton fabric that I stumbled across in **Boyes Department store.** *We were back on track in* **1997***, business good and freshly refurbished and ready for that elusive buyer.*

We sold the Stewart Hotel in 2000 *and commenced our new life, living in our next old house in the countryside – in Ness Cottage at Orchard Lodge, Flixton, the culmination of a shared dream and hard work!*

ANECDOTES:

A Highland Fling

Dreams, challenges and destiny appear to join hands in our lifetime choices. There are often secret forces at work bringing together those who belong together. So, maybe it was not by accident that we came together and entered the challenging world of the hotel trade in the early 1970's. The Proprietor, entrepreneur who fancied a new challenge, and myself, the housekeeper who enjoyed working with people in the front of house situation of a small hotel, were destined to blend together for this role.

During the 1970's, when we began running our small hotel we volunteered to accommodate the entertaining guests for the Benelux Festivals in June. This could be a quiet time of year for business so even though we had to work harder, the income was valued. There was an element of choice if we gaged the price correctly and we had to offer full board in the price structure. The Council paid the account for these entertaining guests of the Town. The New Imperial hotel accommodated the Harlem Flower Girls. These were young pretty Dutch girls all dressed in the same smart matching outfits, and basically, their role was to give the visitors flowers at different venues all over our town - looking pretty and friendly. They were ambassadors not only for the Netherlands but for Scarborough too.

We often had the Dutch bands stay with us and apart from entertaining our town, they entertained us too in our small hotel with impromptu performances each day. One particular band, marched around our Cliff masquerading as horsemen, stopping all the traffic, and then presenting flowers to us. The Dixie Land Jazz Band was my favourite; they were quite spectacular. When they played in the hotel, the music was vibrant, bouncing around the building, filling every orifice. The acoustics of the building were perfect because of the open cantilevered staircase, which was exposed from the entrance hall to the ceiling height of the third floor of bedrooms (after re-building the top floor in 1977).

Therefore, our positive experiences of the bands lingered on and we couldn't imagine these disciplined musicians any other way, but we were soon to be enlightened one Easter in the 1980's.

The Band in question were from Scotland and we were usually very comfortable with these visitors as for many years July had traditionally been a Scottish time. The first two weeks of July were the Edinburgh fortnight and the last two weeks were called the Glasgow fortnight.

Good Friday arrived - a cool spring day with a watery sun. After lunch, our Band stormed the reception, bombarding my peace and literally threw their bags in the hall. On the plus side, their instruments were not thrown in; at least something was of value to them. My face must have expressed how I felt, as the leader said, "She looks frightened of us!" I thought, 'Yes, horrified'. They were your typical skin head stereotype group, wearing ill-fitting short legged jeans, hung with thick elastic braces, exposing 'bovver boots', which were laced to calf level, as well as what appeared to be, steel toecaps, ready for the kicking of a coward's fight. My first thoughts, 'would I sleep tonight; would my neat, fresh- smelling bedrooms survive the rancid smell of this masculinity; would my other visitors book out and leave?' I escorted them to their bedrooms and explained the keys and house rules but I didn't expect them to take any notice. I also knew my husband would be watching them from a distance. Early confrontation was not his style, but I had witnessed his wrath on those who plundered or made mistakes. He had a cool to icy venom, blood drained from his already pale complexion, ready to strike with fist. I always waited with baited breath for the outcome! For the time being, he was just on Watch Duty. He had been a prison officer in Canada in the 1950's, so was trained to be quite cool and cunning. Some situations have to be observed - sometimes you can be pleasantly surprised!

The Band of 12 young men had only booked bed and breakfast, for which I was relieved. Usually, troublesome looking visitors behaved impeccably on their first night and even their second night. It was always the last night they 'let their hair down'. Poor room 22, it had its fair share of troublesome people!

I suppose the reason being it was on the top floor and the occupants probably thought it was way out of sight of the management. There were 6 floors to our beautiful building and no lift. I was described as, "Fit as a mountain goat!" by some visitors simply because I climbed them up and down all day at quite a brisk pace. Some restraint was required conducting visitors for their first time! The same applied to the bandsmen. With all that puffing and blowing their hearts and lungs should have been in good health; except for the fact that they smoked like troopers!

On the morning after the second night, there was a tell-tale sign of the possibilities to come! At about seven o'clock, I opened up the building for the new day and climbed the stairs. I carefully inspected the landings and bathrooms, opening the fire doors and putting night lights out and daytime wall lights on. In that time-period of the 1980's, only six bedrooms were en-suite; other bedrooms shared the three bathrooms. A sweet spinster of fragile disposition, who barely spoke more than two words at a time, and who we also thought was high on Valium, usually booked room seven and shared the bathroom with room eight. Miss Blenkinsop had stayed many times and we always felt quite protective of her. However, we had a breakthrough and after several years she had started calling me by my name, Constance, (she must have been quietly listening to my Mother who lived with us). To my horror, when I checked the shared bathroom for the expected vomit from the occupants of room eight, (bovver boys), what I discovered instead was a gruesome sausage of excreta in the bath. "Oh dear!" I said aloud, "I hope Miss ... hasn't seen this!" Niftily, as a stage magician I grabbed toilet paper and parcelled the offending lump completely and flushed it down the toilet. I then dashed down a floor to the linen cupboard where I stored the cleaning materials, grasped the disinfectant to speedily clean the bath before the other visitors arose to begin morning ablutions. In my opinion, the suspects for the troublesome gesture were in room eight and were still probably fast asleep in their bovver boots dreaming of their first ciggy of the day. Challenges came to us all every day. It was always a good feeling when they were solved quickly.

Late on the last night, I knew my husband had been reading in the kitchen. As I was still awake and when I heard a key in the office lock, I thought to stand behind the door and make him jump as he came in so I waited quietly, (our bedrooms were behind the office). Another key was tried in the lock and at first I thought, 'He must be tired'. But as the fourth key was tried in the lock I realized it was a potential thief and stood there in petrified silence, shaking from head to foot.

There was the jangling and rattling of a large bunch of keys, and frustrated sighs; only by chance, as luck would have it, as they moved on to the bar door next, and applied the same procedure and equally had no success. Some other visitors coming 'home' must have then disturbed them, so they escaped upstairs. My husband never heard a thing!

The next morning, after the third night, time gathered momentum. The boys behaved impeccably at breakfast again, after which the head boy wanted to settle their account. However, I still had a niggling suspicion something was going to either surprise or shock us!

After breakfast was completed and the tables cleaned and re-laid for the next meal, Sandie, my cleaning lady, and I gathered our equipment. We were ready and armed to clean and re-stage the bedrooms ready for the next visitors. We commenced the work on the top floor so logically we could work our way down the building. Sandwiched between the cleaning, I attacked the washing; bed linen was bundled ready for the laundry to collect and I, myself, washed the towels on the premises. These towels were hung on the creel for many hours before being tumbled fluffily, folded, and stacked in the linen room. The rooms were worked in chronological order - 18, 19, 20, 21, and 22. I knew the boys had checked out and left the building but good routine is hard to break, and as I went to knock on the door of room 22, the last on that floor, and before inserting my master key in the lock, it was a shock when the door fell in to the room! The door had been strategically placed and also the door jamb was splintered and torn. This was another job for my Master of maintenance! Don began the task immediately and because of the structure it took two days to complete. First of all, he had to glue and repair the doorjamb. When the glue had hardened, on the second day he re-hung the door. So, although this room had a lovely view, it then became a view of a room, having no door. This created psychological problems for the other visitors residing in rooms on that landing. It must have been very tempting and word spread to the third floor rooms about spares. Remember, this was a very busy Easter week. The room had been ransacked in a way that made me laugh. The televisions in those days were on the whole heavier and more cumbersome to move from room to room. Two people with the strength of Charles Atlas were ideally required for this task. Don had bought a job lot cheap from our Television engineer, who had revamped them from stock abandoned by his other customers. One strong couple decided they liked the television picture better in room 22 rather than their own and must have really struggled to swap them. Other people had run out of refreshments for their courtesy beverage trays and took supplies from room 22. Another couple borrowed the pillows - they must have been sat up in bed asleep! Another couple borrowed the blankets - they must have been cold! The borrowing stopped of course as soon as the door for room 22 was rehung!

In theory, we could have charged the band group for the damage, but we suspected it would be an unnecessary battle and put it down to a life experience and maybe a battle we would never win.

The neighbours in the next room enlightened us later in the day. Apparently, there had been eight 'bovver boys' pushing on the outside of the door to be let in room 22 but the two residing inside the room would not let them in. The man of the neighbouring room peeped out of his room to see what was going on and promptly and sensibly went back in his own and locked the door, where the couple must have slept each with one eye open.

After this eventful Easter, I was a little more cautious about accommodating bands but to be fair they never tried to book again. Maybe, it's the old story, they never stayed in the same place twice because of all the damage they created each time.

When the Cat's away

My darling Mother lived with us in the latter years of her life for 15 years and she was a 'live in' treasure for both the family and the business. In the 1980's, when my husband, Don, travelled away on his NATO exercises with the RNXS, my Mother and I always seemed to have an adventure.

Don made Mother an en-suite bedroom out of a large Victorian bathroom on the 1st floor at the back of the building. It wasn't big enough for a visitor but my Mother was very happy with it. She was extremely adept at making me laugh. When Don and I were busy in Breakfast or Dinner service, she manned the reception and served in the bar before Dinner. Consequently, when she was booking visitors in at Reception in this time period she studied the character types. Along a passage near my Mother's room, was another toilet, which had been the 'shit chute' or dry toilet pre-dating the invention of the water closet. In the 1980's, this small room doubled up as the exit for the fire escape. If the potential visitor looked remotely like an alcoholic drinker, she offered them a room on the next floor up - 2nd floor. "I'm not having drunks walk up and down my passage all night long!" she would quip. This toilet was the nearest for those drinking in the bar, which was on the ground floor.

Once, when Don was away with the Navy, I had three policemen in our bedroom! This transpired in the early hours of the morning as we were awakened by a 'Doing, Doing, Doing' noise on the fire escape. Our bedroom was situated in close proximity of the fire escape so it was not difficult to hear intruders going up. Surprisingly, my Mother even heard it in her 1st floor bedroom overlooking the back yard. As I looked out of the window, I saw a skinny runt of man diving this way and that and he seemed to be uncertain of which way to go. Maybe, I thought, he was looking for a place to hide. I rang the police. "There's an intruder at the back of the Stewart Hotel, running up and down our fire escape." The response came swiftly. "It's all right luv, Palm Court has rung us just before you and said a man had jumped over your eight-foot high gate", which Don had clad with barbed wire on its top as a deterrent. I peeped out of my window onto the fire escape and a thimble full of back yard, where I saw three policemen with torches trying to find this lithesome character. The next sound was that of the doorbell on the main front door of the hotel. Hurriedly, I put on my overcoat to answer the insistent ring. "Ah! Three more policemen." I smiled. They requested to look inside the building. So, I took them to our bedroom, where the event was first witnessed. Our rooms were small - just enough space for a double bed, wardrobe and chest of drawers. Although, we did have an en-suite. It was pretty packed, myself and one policeman stood on the bed peering out of the window, and the other two policemen trying to look busy searching for the man in the en-suite and under the bed! Meanwhile, my Mother had joined us, having armed herself with a poker from the lounge fireplace. She gestured to the policemen, "I'll search upstairs". The police followed her but came down empty handed after about ten minutes.

The policeman with a 'walky talky' said, "We'll have to search the back yard better! The police in the back lane haven't seen him come out." He looked really perplexed. "Is there anything in the yard he can hit us with?" he asked. "Yes there certainly is! There are bottles, wood, coal, metal rods and even dustbin lids!" Eventually, there were six policemen in the back yard furtively hunting in the nooks and crannies. At last, they found him squeezed in a space between the outer wall of the hotel building and the outer wall of the outside toilet, (w.c. not a dry toilet). The space was about 18 inches wide. On being questioned by the police as to what he was doing, he said, "I just climbed over for a piss." (that was a rather extreme journey to take over barbed wire just to go to the toilet). When the police searched in his pockets, there were lots of miniature bottles of alcohol, which we were told he had stolen from a nearby large Hotel.

Another time when Don was away, my Mother made a blunder. We had experienced a busy day, having 30 visitors staying with us, and one member of our team away on Her Majesty's Service. I was tired, (whacked in fact). Mum said, "I'll finish off in the bar. You get yourself off to bed". Our eldest little girl had gone to bed hours earlier, and was fast asleep (the little sweetheart).

Mother must have been whacked herself - she locked all her keys in the bar, including the bar key! She tried knocking on the office door. Nowadays, 2018, we would just ring on a mobile phone. Every one carries a mobile now like a second skin! I was out to the world - in a deep sleep. In the 1980's, we had not adopted the habit of locking the lounge door on a night, which was fortunate. Mum was able to push two crimson fabric upholstered easy chairs together, to create, a 'make shift bed' and tried to sleep in the lounge. This room was on the ground floor overlooking the Cliff and car park. It also had a hypnotic view of the sea and coastline towards Cayton Bay. Although she was very tired, she did not sleep very well at all! This was not surprising. In the early hours of the morning, she witnessed a man passing the lounge door wearing striped pyjamas, (it was a four panelled bevel glass door). She aroused herself from her 'makeshift bed' and staggered towards the lounge window, trying to ascertain if he was sleep walking or fully awake. As it turned out, he was fully awake. We surmised that he was aroused from sleep by a call of nature to spend 'a penny'. He must have looked out of the bedroom window and saw an empty car parking space. As my Mother watched the events through the lounge window, the man disappeared up the Cliff out of sight. Only a few minutes later, he came back to our Cliff and nicely drove into the vacant car space with a happy expression erupting from his face.

Parking had been at a premium in our area of hotels since the 1960's, but most of the hotels were built in an era when the motorcar was not invented. Since obtaining the luxury of personal transport, lots of people liked to park on the Cliff, not only for the convenience of being near their hotels but also for the shops.

The next morning, of course, I released Mother from her torture; she had barely slept a wink!

Then, we had to employ the services of a locksmith to release the bar key from the bar. The irony of this is that one of Don's occupations was a locksmith and he was away!

I called this 'While the Cat's away' because sometimes Don would just be looking at me quite expressionless, and I would say to him, "What are you looking at?" His reply always was "A Cat can look at a King!"

A Bit on the Side

The late 1980's and 1990's were fraught with problems in the finances for most business people. Our problems stemmed in many ways from our building project of a purpose built small hotel in the countryside.
   Winter business was very much lower than summer and generally there wasn't many tourists in winter. One February, we gained four couples for two nights stay. Don was away with RNXS (Royal Navy Auxiliary Service) but my Mother lived with us in the 1980's and relished the idea of being busier than usual. The two Dutch couples, on arrival, told us they were childless by choice and said they didn't think the modern world was suitable for children! The other two couples were from London but with Mediterranean accents. We were very pleased with the extra business. However, the next morning our viewpoint changed. The Dutch couples came down to breakfast and were lovely to look after and chatted away quite happily with us even though their childless ideas had appeared extreme at our first encounter. They seemed to be enjoying our seaside Town. The next to arrive for breakfast were only the ladies of the Mediterranean couples and whilst I was serving them I had to break off to answer a phone call. This was from the police. "Hello, this is the local police... Do you have a Mr. Napoli staying with you?" My simple reply was, "Yes, but they haven't come down to breakfast yet." The police reply surprised me. "They won't be having breakfast with you. They are here with us in jail." There was a bit of a stunned silence from myself. Then, being my usual, thoughtful, self I said "Would you like a word with their wives, they are in the dining room?" Now it was the policeman's turned to be stunned. "Oh, they have women with them? Don't tell them we rang, we will be coming to your place

in a little while." "Shall I ring you when they have gone out?" I said. His reply, "Yes, that's a good idea. Is it alright if we do a search on their rooms?" Now who in their right mind says no to this question from the police! Naturally, I said. "Yes." So it transpired, when the ladies went out, the Drug Squad stormed the hotel! Three burly under cover policemen, one dressed like a hippy and at least 6'6" tall, plus a slim petite undercover police lady. When they searched the first room, the police lady and hippy policeman started hugging and dancing around at their discovery.

Wrapped in what appeared to be cling film, was a solid looking black mass of a product, which they explained to me was cannabis, and estimated a street value of £12,000. The 'Mediterranean's' were doing a little business whilst in town on their holidays and were observed in one of the local pubs trying to sell their wares. Now, the police had found the evidence, they needed a description of the wives. Observation is not my strongest character trait; in fact I drew a blank. But my Mother, enjoying all the activities, gave a brilliant description, long hair, fur coats etc. The Police picked them up outside the main Post Office and took them to jail too! The next to arrive, were the forensic team dusting the rooms for fingerprints and searching for any other evidence. When they had completed their work, which took hours, the room was covered in a fine film of black dust, invading every article.

I had been trained well into being security conscious and started to be concerned about my hotel keys, so I rang the Police. The reply was, "Don't worry. We'll get them to you as soon as possible." The day drifted into evening and still no news about my keys. When I knew the Dutch couples were in the building late at night, I secured the snibs on the main entrance door locks so that the keys would not turn in the locks. If the 'Mediterraneans' came back, it would encourage them to ring the doorbell to attain entrance. After all, their other possessions were stored in our hotel bedrooms.

This eased the tension my Mother and I were experiencing but we decided not to undress for bed. They did not return until shortly after midnight, ringing the doorbell with a long shrill ring! My Mother said "You go up to the rooms with them and if they do anything to you, I'll trip them up at the bottom of the stairs!" She was always a treasure like that - full of funny optimism. I was safe, and they were very apologetic about the circumstances in which they had put us.

On the following day, we commenced the cleaning after forensics, which took two full mornings. The police asked me if I wanted any expenses for all the mess experienced. I declined.

Don would never believe this story when he came home! Something always happened when he was away with the Navy!

A few weeks later, outside Woolworths, by chance I saw the hippy under-cover Drugs Squad Officer. Not difficult to recognise, being 6'6" tall! He told me they turned out to be conmen, so it was not solid cannabis, but a mixture and they were fined £6,000.

Even with all our efforts, by the 1990's our overdraft was growing at £10,000 a year, which seems very modest compared to 2018 but in relative terms it was very unpleasant. Don and I were always thinking of legitimate ways to earn a little extra. Don started working outside the business - painting and decorating and I made jam to sell to our visitors. We had established the building site at Flixton and were loath to put any more borrowed money into the project, which was building our own small hotel with car park! Don set up a new business, where all our extra work endeavours were passed through. He used to go out to Flixton most days but it was mainly gardening and labouring related jobs that cost only his time. In July, he brought home buckets full of Raspberries, which began my jam making days. The hotel was pulling in so little that our eldest daughter acquired a full Grant for University. The extra business we achieved, no matter how unusual, was cherished and we learned to be very tolerant. Not that we weren't before the nineties!

In this time period an optimistic entrepreneurial company was expanding to our Town, opening a retail outlet in the main street. The products were in the cheap price range. Three of the company's operatives were sent to our Town to set this business up, in winter, and decided to use our small hotel as a base. This was for three to four nights per week and for many weeks. The accommodation they required was three rooms for single occupancy. The quote we gave did not have a single room supplement. So, the deal was clinched and intrigue began. The party consisted of two men and one lady. One gentleman was of Arabian descent and I suspected he had not stayed in hotels very often, as he slept between the blankets, not the sheets. I thought my best option was to explain the system of sleeping here, as financially, it was going to work out more expensive. We would have to send the blankets to the laundry every week compared to laundering sheets. Also, I had a painstaking problem to endure and in consequence I had to purchase new eyebrow pluckers. I'd used my own to pluck the hairs off the blankets in which Ali had slept before sending the blankets to the Laundry! Ali was sorted; his was an easy problem to solve. Now, Jill was more complex. Alcohol was her weakness on top of her desire for Jack. It was almost like having two completely different women residing in the hotel.

Our private rooms were behind the reception so hotel life was very accessible, and lots of activity late at night often disturbed us, whether it was verbal or the physical noises of a fight. When our daughters were young, they shared a small room with bunk beds near us so sometimes they awoke to the activities of the night. This room was really a passage, which Don had cleverly adopted for the family. As they grew up, they were allowed their own space; our eldest daughter would probably be 14 years old when she was first allowed her own room on the next floor up. Our youngest daughter at 7 years old by then, logically had her own space too, but remained near us. Both girls really treasured and valued the private space of their bedrooms although the rooms were only small. The expression, 'You couldn't swing a cat round!' was the best way to describe their rooms!

One night shortly before midnight, (my usual time to go to bed), Jill was making use of the residents' payphone in the reception rather noisily, (mobile phones were in their infancy and were the size of a brick for those who could afford them!). I peeped out of the office door and saw Jill who looked a complete mess, hair tangled like a witch, no make-up and day clothes all crumpled. She was as drunk as could possibly be; her language incoherent and she kept falling over. Each time she tried to stand up again. I whispered to Don, "I'd better try and handle this one, she'd probably charge you with assault!" She said "Good Bye" in a very slurred weepy voice to the recipient at the other end of the phone line and then collapsed in a heap on the Tartan carpet. Her room was on the second floor front with a beautiful sea view of the Bay. She had only been sober in the daytime for work, so probably the sea view was wasted and she never noticed it. "Do you need any help getting to your room?" I enquired politely - as if this was just a normal service we offered. "Yesh Pleasesh" she replied. Together we struggled and I managed to stand her up with arms around each other. Then, it was time to attack the stairs! The staircase was Georgian and had a very low bannister rail compared to 20th Century design. I therefore elected to go on the bannister side. I didn't want to lose her over the rail in her drunken stupor! It took us a good 15 minutes to reach her room, where I released her to the open arms of the double bed, or so I thought! As for myself, I went back to bed, certain that adventure over for the night. About half an hour later, we were jolted awake again. I peeped out of the office and there she was on the pay phone again, pleading with the recipient. She was oblivious to me watching, so this time I went back to bed. She could have been at it all night up and down the stairs like a yo-yo; someone had to make a decision. So, I decided, "I'm not playing that game!"

In the morning, she appeared a glamorous lady with an air of efficiency. There was nothing about her demeanour that hinted that she had been a total drunk the night prior. She wore a perfect light grey suit, the make-up was on and the hair well fashioned. She appeared to be a very efficient Jekyll and Hyde. The only clues were in the bedroom, clothes strewn all over the floor, several empty wine bottles scattered around and a noticeable dint in the wall. Jack on the other hand had a more stable character but obviously enjoyed a good dollop of romance whilst working away from home. His bed was never slept in, but he must have slept somewhere. But where indeed!

Lock up your daughters!

It had rained constantly for what appeared to be many weeks - though in reality it was only twelve days. The air was muggy and damp and with that the gardens a rich emerald shade of green. I closed my eyes in quiet contemplation and in a whisper I said a tiny prayer. "Please God? Don't let it rain this weekend? Not for the Golf Society booking! Amen."

My prayer was answered. Friday arrived with the bright chirpy songs of the birds, obviously pleased to see the back of the rain too!

We, that is, my morning cleaning lady Sandie and I, busied ourselves cleaning and staging the bedrooms after the departure of the mid-week bookings (very few because of the rain). Henry, the one-eyed smiling vac, was stashed away in the store cupboard resting for another day. It was just a matter of waiting for the new arrivals.

Don, my husband, chef extraordinaire and chief maintenance man, took advantage of the tides and decided to go sailing with Colin - a decorator friend. Thus, leaving the hotel in "my capable hands" he said with a hearty laugh!

The hotel was tranquil yet my nerves were restless knowing, that when the golfers arrived my every moment would be harnessed!

I sneaked downstairs to prepare myself an aromatic cup of coffee to refresh my tattered nerves. I no sooner had made it when there was a loud prolonged shrill ring on the door bell! "Oh no! They are here already!" I shrieked. I dashed up the stairs from the kitchen with my usual haste. It took about 10 seconds, well timed, after about 20 years of regular habits!

The entrance lobby and pavement were filled with an audience of golf clubs - strewn in random order. The men were dressed, as only team sportsmen would, matching trousers and club motto sweatshirts. They were charging from car to car, with frantic arms flying out like eagles ready for prey. They were on the hunt but only for car parking spaces.

"Yes! Can I help you?" I said, trying to be brave - as if I couldn't tell who they were! The deluge moved forward deliberately not disclosing their names but I was one step ahead! Professionally, I had telephoned the organiser the previous evening and had him refresh me of any name changes. In a quiet moment, I had prepared the registration slips accordingly. Their task was to write their own addresses and car registrations. What a fuss some people make at this small task!

At last they were booked in, keys explained in a flurry. The army drove up my tartan carpeted stairs to my neat fresh smelling bedrooms.

Within 10 minutes, the exodus were racing up the street to the nearest pub as if it were near closing time. It was only 7.00 p.m. The house drifted back to its normal tranquil self...but for how long?

The evening meandered along at a gentle pace. Our other visitors wandered in and out, pausing for a friendly chat, unaware of the night's intrigue to come. The golfers came back infrequently in singular fashion and were surprisingly courteous. 'Maybe.' I thought aloud we would survive after all.

By twelve o'clock midnight, I was depleted and ready for sleep. Don volunteered to perform the late-night guard duty. He was quite happy to read his book in the kitchen until the early hours of the morning - dosing himself with endless cups of tea.

I walked the five flights of stairs, checking the nooks and crannies, closing the fire doors and putting the main lights out. The semi darkness was consoling and peaceful. Some of the other visitors had already gone to bed. Their rhythmic snoring echoed across the landings.

There was a certain satisfaction to having completed the day, having fulfilled our visitors needs and expectations - a job well done.

I slipped into sleep easily. Sleep was not usually a problem for me. But extreme noises in the night always gripped my attention. Sitting me bolt upright, like a robot plugged into an electric current.

After about three hours, the noises began. The 'rabble rousers' sauntered into our haven of peace as if it were three o'clock in the afternoon - not after midnight! "Hello Jack! Is Jim in yet?" They bellowed up our open cantilevered staircase. "Whose turn is it next? Oh, is it Bill's? Where is she? I'm knackered, I wish she'd hurry up! I'm 'deeing' to get to bed!" They had strong South Yorkshire accents.

Don too could not sleep through this torrent of conversation. He decided he had better investigate and try if possible to turn their bellows into whispers. He said to me, "All the other visitors will be coming out of their rooms to investigate too!" He tried to quieten them but it was without success. They could not hear Don for the excitement in their own minds!

Don slipped quietly upstairs - stealthily searching for answers. This was without difficulty in all that ranting and raving. He could not believe his eyes! It appeared to be a production of a music hall farce - naked men running from room to room - totally oblivious to Don's presence. As he looked up the staircase to a higher landing, he saw a young woman cautiously gazing down, who was not one of our customers. "Hey! Who are you?" he demanded. The fleeting figure dashed down a passage clothed in an ill-fitting Gaberdine Mac, with a titillating handful of soft pink flesh peeping out.

Don abandoned ship. There was nothing constructive he could think of to do. He could not reason with these men, challenged by excessive alcoholic drink and recreational sex firmly embedded in their thoughts. "Let nature take its course!" he announced. He threw his hands up in submission and escaped to bed. To me, he whispered, "Don't worry it will all go quiet soon when she's performed her role!"

Gradually, over the next half hour, the house drifted back into quiet again. The mysterious figure seemed to disappear - being absorbed into the very fabric of the building. Whoever she was, she certainly quelled their excitement and allowed the rest of us the bliss of sleep.

Dawn arrived in a hurry. Growls of contented snores bounced around the bedroom landings as I put the lights on for the day. I wondered if they would have an appetite for a Full English Breakfast?

The routine of preparing the "en place" for breakfast was completed. There was just enough time for a leisurely bowl of Branflakes laced with ice cold milk - before our little soldiers descended the red and gold carpeted stairs for breakfast. The dining room was in the lower ground floor. It was the servants' hall many years ago and still retained an intimate cosy atmosphere. I'm sure many evenings were spent in the candlelight chattering about those upstairs.

Breakfast is by far the best meal of the day. The aroma of bacon sizzling in the pan and fresh ground coffee wafting upstairs, penetrating each bedroom door, was inviting each occupant to rise from slumber.

Amazingly, our middle of the night revellers, were the first down to breakfast!

For my own convenience, I lead the golfers to two enormous mahogany round tables. These gave good elbow room for even the most rotund of them. They helped themselves to mountain peaks of cereal and generous goblets of cool refreshing orange juice. "Full Breakfasts all round Luv!" grinned the one who looked like an Adonis. I thought to myself, 'better give them extra toast, tea and coffee too! Can't have them going off for the day hungry. They certainly know how to work up an appetite!'

I raced to serve such avid sportsmen. They ate quicker than shipwrecked victims entrapped for weeks on a dessert island!

Our other guests came down in 'dribs and drabs', (thankfully) but each gave the golfers a cold hard stare. One brave lady of generous proportions and obviously used to handling little boys without their mums confronted them, "Was it you lot at 3.30 this morning banging and carrying on? Don't you ever sleep?" "No Luv it wasn't us!" said the confident Adonis. "But you can bang on my door any time!" The other men laugh at the clever joke. Adonis whispered to them, "I wouldn't let her in though!"

Within what seems moments of this chastising conversation, the golfers fled. They obviously eat to live - not live to eat. They excitedly loaded their limousines and escaped to golf; the night's recreation clearly in the past.

One of the wives of the golfers rang us in the afternoon. "How are they doing? Are they behaving?" I didn't have the heart to tell her about the night's events, maybe he would tell her at home! My reply to her, "Everything is OK. I think they are having a good time!" No doubt, I think. With a wry smile, we will have more of the same tonight, but just perhaps in a different order! I said aloud, "But, I do hope they all behave tonight and let us get our beauty sleep!"

A couple of days later, amongst the mail delivered, was a miniature brown envelope, on the back of which was hand written 'sender Royal hotel'. Curiosity was a major factor enticing me to open this cute little brown envelope. Inside it was a business card, clearly from a lady in business. It was expertly written, 'Speciality - married men. Please place in your Foyer.' I have to confess, I never displayed it in the Foyer. However, I saved it in the office for a while, just in case there was another desperate customer!

Our daughters were about fifteen and eight years old respectively at the time and knew all about the rumpus in the night - hence the expression of "lock up your daughters". The younger one was not as aware of the implications as was our older one. Fortunately, innocence just made our little one giggle.

The nearly Murder on the top floor!

Seasons came in well-ordered precision, yet each year was different, and each Bank Holiday had its own character mirrored in its people.

One Bank Holiday in spring, we were kept very active. It had been a hard day conducting visitors up and down our five flights of stairs like the Grand old Duke of York; showing a variety of couples our bedrooms available. I relied on instinct to show them what I thought they might like. Many times over the years, I had tried asking them, "What sort of a room are you after?" Usually, the minimum of reply was given, "A double with a sea view". Only the intricacies of needs and choices were left in the depths of their minds. 'Joe Public', some days was quite discriminating on what he would accept for a room, in dimensions, layout of furniture, bed size, and even colour schemes. An example of colour scheme, was one time when we were very busy on the reception desk and one of my teenage daughters offered to take someone up to view a room available for accommodation. The man of the couple said, "Where is the switch to turn the colour down? Do you provide sunglasses?" 'Ah! A comedian!' thought my daughter. The wallpaper in this particular room was 1970's style paisley pattern pink and yellow, and we thought it was lovely, but we learnt over the years that plain is best.

That Saturday was one of those discriminating days and although we still had two rooms unoccupied, we thought we had done well. This was incredible considering the fussy potential visitors, who had been ringing the doorbell all day!

A friend, Bert, and his wife Jean had called for a drink in the evening, and a chat in our cosy Stewart Tartan bar.

This helped to relax us after the hectic day. Bert had a colourful South Yorkshire accent and always made me laugh about the antics Don and himself got up to in their Army days. My Grandfather's clock struck 12.00 midnight, which coincided with the rumble and screams that bombarded our eardrums; the sound building up to a crescendo down our open cantilevered bedroom staircase. We could not help but hear the thunderous footsteps and their voices squealing, screeching and screaming, craving attention. 'Whatever next!' was my first thought. As if to answer my own question, two twenty-year old women clad in fleecy pyjamas, tussled hair and no makeup, howled, "There's a man trying to kill a woman in the room next to ours on the top floor!" The top floor was the fourth floor of bedrooms and sixty-foot up from the basement level. The latter housed the kitchen and dining room. Don, my husband, Bert and myself were the obvious volunteers to investigate these allegations. We left Jean on guard duty in the bar; surely she would be safe in there?

Our small platoon mounted the stairs ready to engage the enemy, or whatever else we might encounter. The invention of the mobile Freeway phone was a must in times of action in the early 1990's and in such instances my role became the signalman, (or to be politically correct nowadays, the signal person). We really did not know what we would encounter. On reaching the top floor with a band of ever growing stragglers, like iron filings clinging to magnets; all curious in search of a holiday adventure. This was something to talk about when they returned home. We had to identify the bedroom first, and because all was quiet, we were at a momentary loss for direction. It had to be a process of elimination with 4 en suite bedrooms on that floor. The stars twinkled down on us from the skylight. The seagulls called to one another, but never gave a clue. Don knocked on the door, of what he thought was the primary target. The response was not what he had anticipated. "It's not us in here," chirped two gentle voices in harmony. The next room was correct. Don bellowed into the silence, "If you don't give up in there, I'm going to have to come in!" That was a laugh for a start. If one of them had put the snib down on the latch lock, there was no way Don could have turned his Master key. But, he had to take command of the situation and show them authority. I was not going to encourage him to climb on the roof, up the ladder and through the hatch in the store cupboard. Then he would have to sidle down to the window and force entry about sixty foot up from street level and whilst balancing on the low parapet wall! (It was the sidling down to the window and balancing that discouraged me). Even though Don had been a painter and decorator for his first trade and certainly had a head for heights, I was not good on taking that sort of chance! However, there was a reply. A soft female voice said, "I'm alright, really". The man never spoke. So there were two possible assumptions open to us, either she had been trying to kill him and he was already laid there stone dead or she was telling the truth and he was quietly trembling in fear at the thought of Don's possible confrontation becoming a reality. We waited in silence, all fifteen of us for at least 60 seconds. Our band of followers, eyes darting from one to another in horror yet recognizing our leadership, so stood loyally still. Don signalled like a conductor of a symphony. They were a disciplined group at the ready for any instructions displayed. We retreated to the next landing, where we discussed in whispers and eased the fears of those around us, calming the situation. Kristina, our regular Swedish guest in room 15, peeped out at us, "Is everything alright Connie? Do you need any help?" I signalled in mime that we had the situation under control and we were "OK"; this is an internationally known expression and had been suitable for all our foreign travellers! We decided there was nothing else to do but defuse the situation and recommended all to go to bed, except Don who decided to wait up for the next stage of events, if any occurred. Most of the worries were supposition not fact.

My husband was totally addicted to reading novels and dosing himself with cups of tea, often until 2.00 and 3.00 in the morning. We were a good blend as I took over the early breakfasts and departures. So, for Don staying up late was not a new problem and being a chef, he was quite at home in the basement kitchen next to his beloved

Benham oven. There, he was able to hear the noises of the night of people walking up and down the staircase. The design of the staircase enabled these noises to drift around the building and be captured by any restless sleeper or avid reader. At about 2.00 a.m, he heard downward footsteps. My husband had never been a good runner, not even at school. Put him in a yacht in the middle of an ocean and he would find his way safely home. Consequently, by the time he reached the ground floor and walked to the lounge window, he just caught a glimpse of our female walking up to the top of the street. With a certain amount of relief, yet still anxious, he thought well at least she is still alive. Even the 'Sandman' eventually captured Don, so he toddled off to bed. Some things can only be sorted out in daylight.

The closing details of this escapade came together with a little detective work during Breakfast service. Our cute harmonious couple in the "wrong" room could not wait to tell us. "She came back you know at about 4.00 a.m. but he would not let her in; she tried with her key, but could not get it to turn. We've heard him coughing this morning, so he is alive!"

The young man was certainly the last person we expected to come down to breakfast. The embarrassment of it! All eyes would be peering at him whilst he tried to eat breakfast. He tiptoed out of the building whilst everyone else was enjoying the best meal of the day. But he did not leave the keys! I panicked momentarily (a female Pummell trait), until reason took over. I wrote that day a questing type letter to the name and address given on the registration slip, putting in a thoughtfully place stamp addressed envelope. "Dear Miss... You left this morning in rather a hurry and inadvertently forgot to leave our keys. Would you be kind enough to return them to us?" She took the cue and returned the keys in a few days. The night key for the front door was in fine fettle, but the bedroom key was spiralled into a design that even Henry Moore would have been proud of!

The evidence of the night's events was displayed clearly in their bedroom. Sandie and I were eager to inspect the bedroom. On entering the bedroom, it was very obvious to us there had been an enormous battle. The bed lay crippled on the floor, balancing precariously on the three remaining legs out of six. Great clumps of black hair spread across the white blood-spattered sheets; so much hair that one of them surely had a bald patch. This must have been difficult to hide for the return journey home that day. At its peak, it must have been a ferocious fight and have been very worrying for the neighbours. It was doubtful as to whether this young couple would be return visitors for another year! As for Jean, she nearly fell asleep in the bar whilst waiting for us to return and missed most of the action.